Excavations at 25 Cannon Street, City of London

From the Middle Bronze Age to the Great Fire

Nicholas J Elsden

MoLAS Archaeology Studies Series 5

Museum of London Archaeology Service

MoLAS Archaeology Studies Series

1 A 14th-century pottery site in Kingston upon Thames, Surrey: excavations at 70–76 Eden Street, Pat Miller and Roy Stephenson
ISBN 1 901992 07 1

2 Excavations at 72–75 Cheapside/83–93 Queen Street, City of London, Julian Hill and Aidan Woodger
ISBN 1 901992 08 X

3 Bankside: excavations at Benbow House, Southwark, London SE1, Anthony Mackinder and Simon Blatherwick
ISBN 1 901992 12 8

4 A Romano-British cemetery on Watling Street: excavations at 165 Great Dover Street, Southwark, London, Anthony Mackinder
ISBN 1 901992 11 X

5 Excavations at 25 Cannon Street, City of London: from the Middle Bronze Age to the Great Fire, Nicholas J Elsden
ISBN 1 901992 22 5

Published by the Museum of London Archaeology Service

Production and series design by Tracy Wellman
Typesetting and design by Susan Banks
Reprographics by Andy Chopping
Editing by Monica Kendall
Series editing by Sue Hirst/Susan M Wright

Printed by the Lavenham Press

Front cover: the author examining a complete pot found beneath the floor of a 12th-century cellared building; 18th-century tin-glazed wall tile; a collapsed Roman tessellated floor; the new development at 25 Cannon Street

CONTRIBUTORS

Principal author	Nicholas J Elsden
Prehistoric pottery	Louise Rayner
Roman pottery	Robin Symonds
Late Saxon/medieval and later pottery	Lyn Blackmore
Ceramic building material	Ian M Betts
Non-ceramic finds	Jackie Keily
Struck flint	Jonathan Cotton
Animal remains	Alan Pipe
Botanical remains	Lisa Gray
Graphics	Caroline Caldwell, Helen Jones, Kate Pollard, Anthony Sibthorpe
Photography	Edwin Baker, Andy Chopping, Margaret Cox
Project managers	Nick Bateman, Peter Rowsome
Editors	Monica Kendall, Peter Rowsome

CONTENTS

FIGURES

TABLES

SUMMARY

This report presents the results of an excavation and associated fieldwork at 25 Cannon Street, in the City of London, carried out by the Museum of London Archaeology Service (MoLAS) between 1996 and 1999, under site code CAO96. Key findings from the excavation included Middle Bronze Age pottery, late 1st-century buildings and four cellared buildings dating from the 11th century. This report incorporates the observations made on the site by Ivor Noël Hume of the Guildhall Museum in advance of the construction of Gateway House in 1954. These were published by John Shepherd in 1986, and have been assigned the site code GM160. Some interpretations of the 1954 records are revised here in the light of the new data. The centre of the site lies at national grid reference TQ 3224 8107.

The earliest archaeological evidence found was an assemblage of redeposited Middle Bronze Age pottery (period 1). The identification of both bucket and globular urns in the Deverel-Rimbury tradition suggests occupation in the general vicinity of the site during this period.

The site lies on the southern slopes of the western of two hills on which the Roman and later city was built, and for the first five or ten years after the Roman conquest in AD 43 the site lay on the underutilised margins of the new city. The earliest phase of Roman construction (period 2), which may not have taken place until after AD 60, was accompanied by quarrying for gravel and brickearth (OA2). Early occupation was characterised by buildings with timber sill beams (B1–3), and was followed by increasingly dense development from *c* AD 70 (period 3), with the introduction of masonry buildings as well as new timber structures.

Around AD 100 the first building with masonry walls (B100) was demolished to make way for a larger structure (B10) whose orientation differed from that of earlier buildings, but was reflected in buildings extending some 100m to the east. By *c* AD 140–250 the area had become densely built up (period 4), with some buildings on the eastern side of the site possessing tessellated floors of relatively crude workmanship (B14–15). The consistent alignment of buildings on the northern edge of the site, and at Watling House to the east, has been used to hypothesise the route of a Roman road immediately to the north, beneath Watling Street, but a little further north than previously suggested.

At least one of the 2nd-century buildings was demolished in the 3rd century to make way for a building with extensive tessellated floors (B21), which continued in use, with declining standards of repair, until the end of Roman occupation (period 5). On the northern side of the site a building was constructed in the 3rd or 4th century (B20) with an orientation that differs from other buildings, and may reflect a change in alignment of the hypothesised road. Notable among the Roman finds was part of a 3rd- or 4th-century stone mould, thought to be for the manufacture of decorated pewter plates. The abandonment of the site at the end of the Roman occupation cannot be adequately dated, but is marked by the accumulation of 'dark earth' over the floors (period 6).

The site was reoccupied in the 10th or 11th century, and by the mid 11th century four buildings with timber-lined cellars had been constructed (period 7). Their construction apparently predates that of Friday Street and the church of St Werburga, later St John the Evangelist. One building had two whole pots buried beneath its floor, either as an offering, or perhaps for an industrial purpose. Two crucibles and a Roman tile reworked as a mould for copper-alloy ingots demonstrate a degree of industrial activity in the vicinity during this period.

The dating of Friday Street is equivocal: the earliest road surface observed may have been constructed in the late 11th century, or may have dated to after 1180 (period 8). Earlier deposits are likely to have been preserved *in situ* beneath this. The church of St Werburga was established between 1098 and 1108, and was rebuilt with a wider chancel in the 13th or 14th century (B103).

Evidence for medieval and later buildings was heavily truncated by modern basements, but suggested that early medieval buildings stretched back a standard distance of *c* 12.5m on either side of Friday Street, similar to that of other medieval buildings in the vicinity (periods 8–9). The majority of the medieval evidence took the form of rubbish and cesspits. Some of the latter were constructed with masonry walls from the 13th century onwards.

Cellars and more cesspits attest occupation up to the Great Fire of 1666 (period 10), which devastated the whole site. The church of St John the Evangelist was not rebuilt, but the churchyard continued in use as a burial ground until the 19th century (period 11).

ACKNOWLEDGEMENTS

MoLAS would like to thank 25 Cannon Street Ltd for their generous funding of the fieldwork and publication of the excavations at 25 Cannon Street, and especially Chris Tibble for his help and support throughout the project.

Particular thanks go to John Pearson of EC Harris Project Management, John Price of RHWL Architects, and Andy Routledge of Henry Demolition.

David Whipp, archaeological consultant of Mills Whipp Partnership, monitored the fieldwork on behalf of 25 Cannon Street Ltd.

Thanks also go to site managers Rob Ware and Tom Henry of Henry Demolition, and Peter Galbraith, Paul Stanley and particularly engineer Kish Desai of Tarmac, as well as Bob McClean of Watermans and Lee Horsely of O'Keefe Construction Ltd for their cooperation and assistance throughout the archaeological projects, which contributed materially to the completion of the excavation.

We would also like to thank Kathryn Stubbs, Senior Planning and Archaeology Officer of the City of London, for her input and support of this project.

The author is grateful to John Shepherd, Catherine Maloney and Alan Thompson, Records Officers of the Museum of London Archaeological Archive, for access to and assistance with the archives from the 1954 fieldwork.

The evaluation was supervised by David Bowsher, conducted by him and Lesley Dunwoodie, Ian Grainger and John Percival, and managed by Bill McCann. The excavation and watching brief were supervised by Nicholas Elsden and Al Steele, managed by Nick Bateman, and conducted by Neil Adams, Ros Aitken, Jeremy Bell, John Binns, Aidan Burford, Howard Burkhill, Steve Chew, Nathalie Cohen, Bob 'The Badger' Cowie, Jessica Cowley, Lorraine Darton, Heather Daunt, Andy Daykin, Ben Eaton, Val Griggs, Lucy Hall, Sarah Hemley, Richard Hewett, Nick Holder, Richard Hoyle, Karl Hulka, Richard Lee, David Mackie, Gordon Malcolm, Mandy Marshall, Mike Parker, Matthew Reynolds, Shaun Richardson, Niall Roycroft, Dave Saxby, Norena Shopland, Dan Swift, Jon Sygrave, Arthur Taylor-Nottingham, Pete Thompson, Jo Wainwright and Thomas Wilson.

The site was surveyed by Steve Every, Duncan Lees, David Mackie and Kate Pollard, and the plans digitised by Dave Bentley and Mark Burch. The site photography was undertaken by Margaret Cox, and the finds were photographed by Edwin Baker and Andy Chopping. Metal detecting was undertaken by Steve Chew of MoLAS, Don Ramsey, and by Ken Bellinger, Ron Hooper and Tony Pilson of the Society of Thames Mudlarks.

Nick Bateman has provided overall project management, Gordon Malcolm programme management, and Peter Rowsome post-excavation management, advice on the form and content of the publication, and editorial assistance.

In addition to the contributors, the finds were assessed by Nigel Jeffries, Susan Pringle and Roberta Tomber, all of Museum of London Specialist Services (MoLSS), and by Kieron Heard of MoLAS. Mike Hammerson identified and dated the Roman coins. Thanks are due to John Shepherd and Angela Wardle of MoLSS for their comments and help in identifying the registered finds. David Dungworth of the Centre for Archaeology carried out the X-ray fluorescence analysis. Conservation was carried out by Dana Goodburn-Brown, Kirsten Suenson-Taylor and Elizabeth Barham, of MoLSS. Faunal remains were assessed by Jane Liddle of MoLSS, and the other assessments were conducted by the specialist contributors from MoLSS.

The summary was translated into French by Dominique de Moulins and into German by Friederike Hammer. The index was compiled by Susanne Atkin.

1

Introduction

1.1 Location and circumstances of fieldwork

This publication reports on the archaeological evaluation, excavation and watching brief conducted at 25 Cannon Street in the City of London. These were recorded under Museum of London archaeological site code CAO96. The site is located on the northern side of Cannon Street, immediately to the east of New Change. It is bounded by Watling Street to the north, and by Bread Street to the east (Fig 1; Fig 2). The site covers an area of approximately 695 sq m, and its centre is located at national grid reference TQ 3224 8107.

During the construction of Gateway House on the site in 1954, the groundworks were monitored by Ivor Noël Hume of the Guildhall Museum, who had also examined the site of the church of St John the Evangelist following clearance of the graveyard. The records and artefacts are held in the Museum of London Archaeological Archive, under site code GM160. The Roman features seen in this work were subsequently published by John Shepherd (1986), and both those and the significant medieval and later features have been integrated into this report.

A new building was proposed in the early 1990s, with more extensive basements and foundations than Gateway House, and a desk-based archaeological assessment indicated that the development would have a potential impact upon archaeological deposits. This development was carried out by 25 Cannon Street Ltd, who generously funded the subsequent archaeological fieldwork and publication. An archaeological evaluation conducted in 1996 confirmed the presence of Roman, medieval and post-medieval remains on the site. Planning consent for the redevelopment at 25 Cannon Street was granted in 1998 subject to a condition which required the implementation of a programme of archaeological works. A rolling programme of excavation, following the demolition of individual areas of the site, was conducted from 22 July to 23 October 1998, during which time watching briefs were also conducted in other parts of the site. During the early stages of the watching brief in the eastern part of the site (Fig 3), it rapidly became apparent that there was a considerably greater depth of significant archaeological deposits present than had been suggested by the evaluation and 1954 watching brief. Consequently, an open area excavation was organised for that part of the site which would be removed during the construction of lift shafts and a crane base. A final watching brief to record deposits exposed during construction ran intermittently until 20 May 1999. The records and finds from the excavation have been deposited with the Museum of London Archaeological Archive, under site code CAO96.

Archaeological deposits have been preserved *in situ* beneath certain areas of the new development, in particular under the southern half of the former Friday Street, where it is expected that Late Saxon road surfaces seal an undisturbed sequence of Roman construction. These are likely to hold the key to the date at which Friday Street was established. In addition,

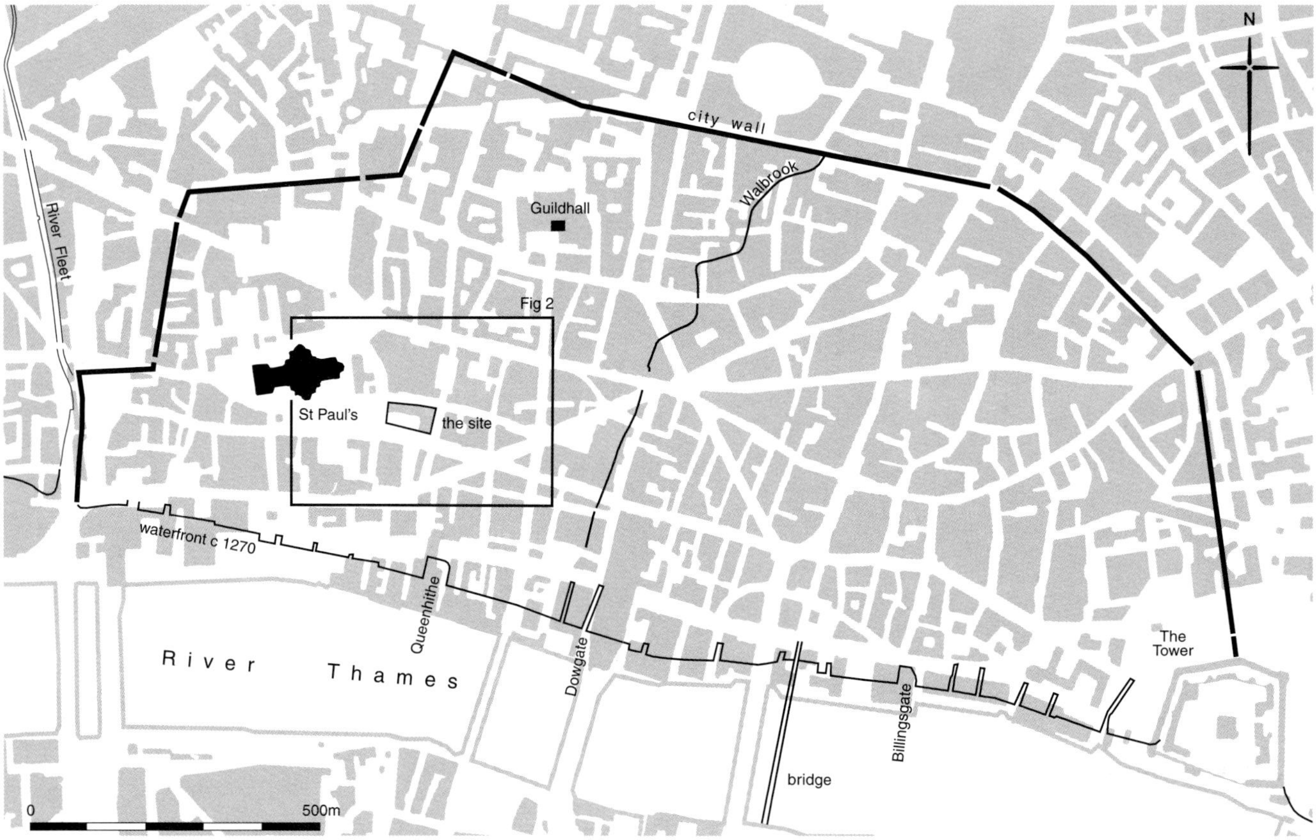

Fig 1 Map showing the location of the site (general), 1:12,500

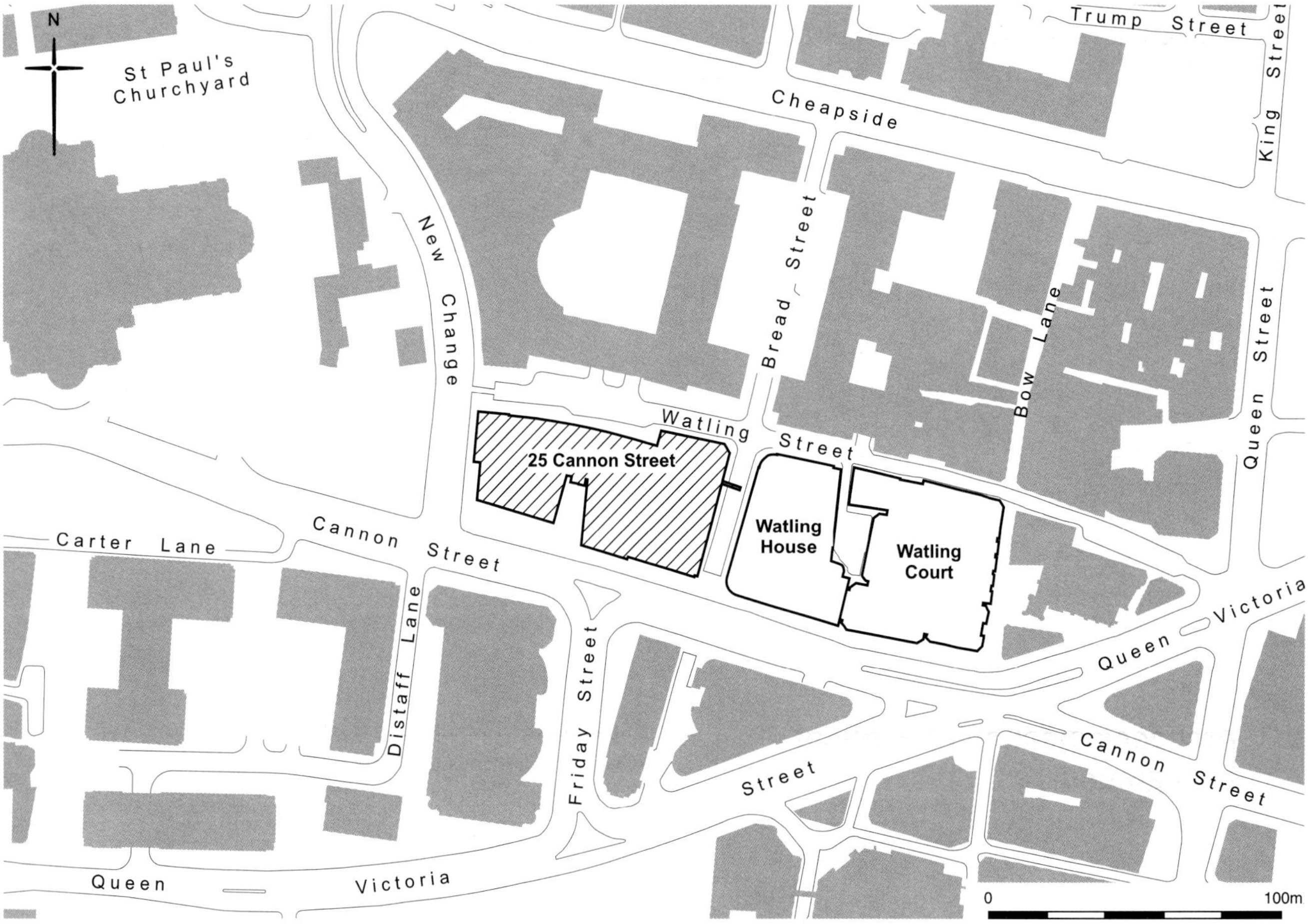

Fig 2 Map showing the location of the site (detail), 1:2,500

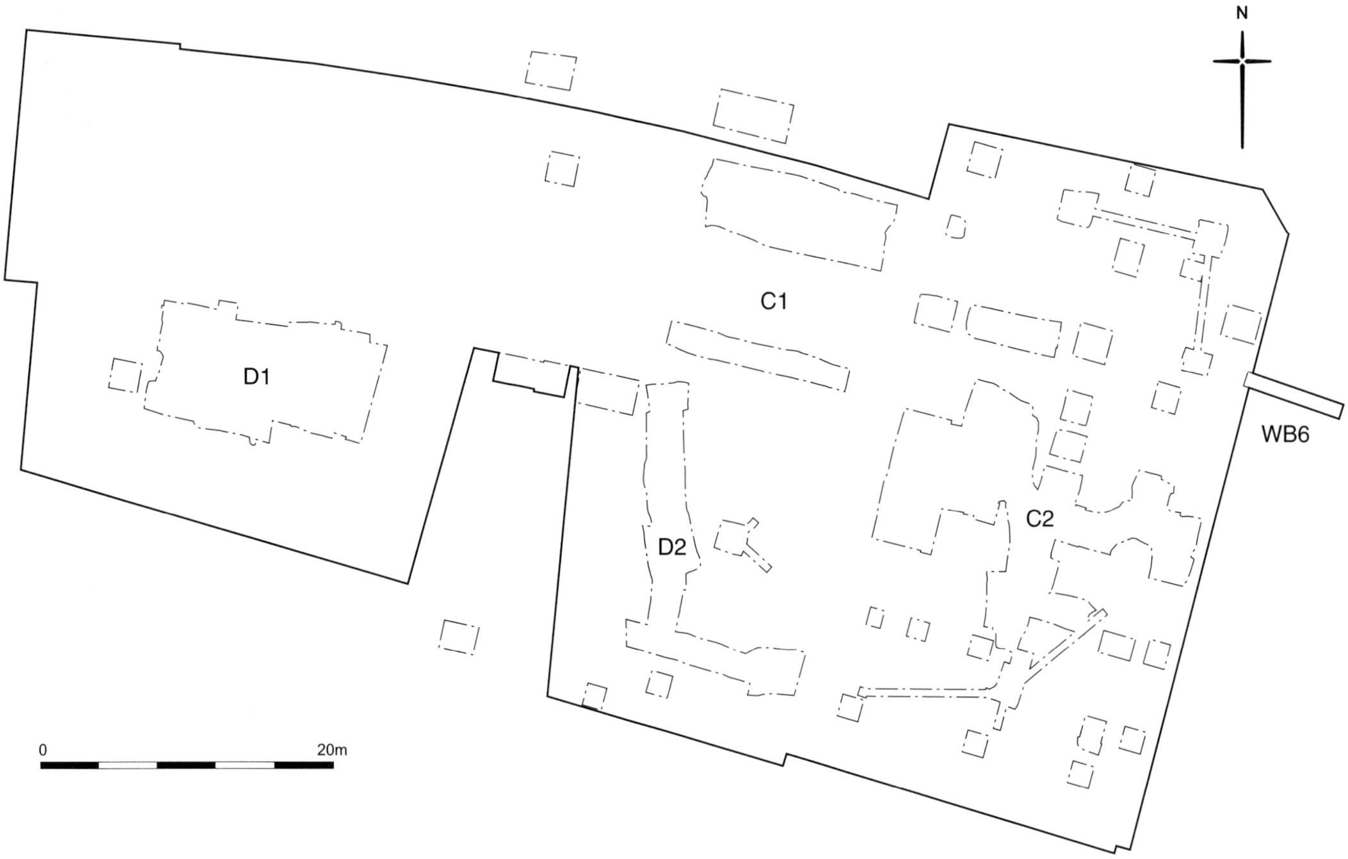

Fig 3 Plan showing the location of the trenches and watching brief areas (unlabelled areas are WB1–5 and testpits 1–6), 1:500

deposits have been preserved over parts of the area to the east of Friday Street, where they have not been either excavated in advance of the new building, or removed by earlier construction.

1.2 Geology and topography

25 Cannon Street is situated on the southern slope of the low hill which lies to the west of the Walbrook stream. Here the London Clay is overlain by floodplain gravels of the Second Thames Terrace, which are capped by varying depths of brickearth. The modern ground surface slopes down to the south towards the River Thames and to the south-east to the Walbrook, from 16.77m OD at Watling Street to 16.45m OD at Cannon Street, and from 17.27m OD at New Change to 16.06m OD at Bread Street.

1.3 Archaeological and historical background

Only scattered evidence of prehistoric activity has been recovered from the area of what would later become the Roman city of Londinium (Merriman 1987), and clear evidence for occupation sites is, so far, lacking.

The Roman city of Londinium covered two low hills bisected by the Walbrook, a stream which flowed southwards into the Thames (see Fig 1); the site lies close to the top of the western hill. Archaeological excavations at Watling Court in 1978, 60m to the east of the site, revealed that a major development had taken place before AD 100 and provides one of the most complete records of domestic buildings recovered from the city (Perring and Roskams 1991, 26–43). These are supplemented by the records from the watching briefs conducted in advance of the construction of Gateway House and the adjacent Watling House in 1954. The Roman sequence from these observations has been published previously (Shepherd 1986).

Initial Roman activity at Watling Court was confined to quarrying brickearth for construction. After levelling the ground with brickearth, a number of buildings were constructed, separated by alleyways, with a major phase of construction between *c* AD 70 and 120. The character of the buildings suggests a residential district. After an extensive fire identified with the Hadrianic fire of *c* AD 125, the area was redeveloped, and the replacement buildings represent the last main phase of Roman construction surviving on that site. Eventually, a deposit of 'dark earth' accumulated across the area, representing a change in land use or an abandonment of the area. The sequence at Watling House was similar to that from Watling Court.

With the exception of the foundation of St Paul's Cathedral in AD 604, there is no evidence of Early Saxon occupation in the area of 25 Cannon Street, as the focus of settlement had shifted to the west of the Roman city. Bread Street (see Fig 2) appears to date from the 9th century, as part of the new Alfredian street grid providing access from Cheapside to the Thames. A group of pits at Watling Court dated to the late 9th or 10th century, and were followed by timber-lined sunken-floored buildings dating from the 10th to 11th centuries; similar buildings are known from the surrounding area (Horsman et al 1988, 21–32).

In the late 11th or 12th century the church of St Werburga, later St John the Evangelist, was established, on the corner of Friday Street – which is documented from the 12th century – and Aethelingestraete, modern Watling Street – documented from the 13th century.

The essentials of the medieval pattern of occupation continued until the devastation of the Great Fire of 1666, vividly described by the diarist John Evelyn: 'Wattling-streete now flaming and most of it reduc'd to ashes' (de Beer 1955, 454). Subsequently the church of St John the Evangelist was not rebuilt, but its site remained in use as a burial ground until the 19th century. Distaff Lane and Little Friday Street ran east–west to the south of the site; in 1852 these were widened to form the westwards extension of Cannon Street. The buildings on the site suffered severe bomb damage in 1941, but were not rebuilt until 1954, with the construction of Gateway House, which straddled a pedestrian route on the approximate line of the former Friday Street.

1.4 Organisation of this report

This report forms part of the MoLAS Archaeology Studies Series. The series is primarily intended to facilitate production of archaeological reports for the London region by working closely in association with local and regional societies. The series aims to present smaller or medium-scale archaeological investigations, sometimes as single-site sequences and at other times with more than one site being linked by broad chronological or subject-matter themes. The series is further designed to link with the MoLAS Monograph Series, through consistent use of format and design. MoLAS would welcome any comments on the design and content of this series.

The arrangement of each volume in the Studies Series will follow a similar order, where, for each site involved, the circumstances of the investigation(s) precede a chronological narrative (Chapter 2) divided where appropriate by archaeological 'period' and land-use entities (see 1.5 below). Specialist analyses are integrated within the text where possible. To avoid disrupting the flow of the text, some of the necessary 'technical support' for conclusions and interpretations has been removed from the thematic chapters and is presented in Chapter 4. Further data that were not considered suitable for publication in this volume, or for which space is not available, are held in the various Research Archives (see below).
A discussion section (Chapter 3) develops the analysis of the principal foci of the site(s), and is followed (Chapter 4) by supporting Specialist appendices on the finds and environmental remains retrieved from the site. Expansion codes for the pottery forms, fabrics and decoration can also be found in Chapter 4.

The nature and quantity of material from the site placed constraints upon the level of detail that could be included in this report. In accordance with the principles laid out in the *Management of archaeological projects* (*MAP* 2, English Heritage 1991), analysis of the material from the recent and 1950s' fieldwork on the site resulted in a series of specialist Research Archives, all.of which are lodged with the Museum of London Archaeological Archive under site codes CAO96 and GM160, and may be consulted by prior arrangement.

1.5 Textual and graphical conventions in this report

The basic unit of cross-reference throughout the archive that supports this report is the context number. This is a unique number given to each archaeological event on site (such as a layer, wall, pit cut, road surface etc). Context numbers in the text are shown thus: [100]. Accession numbers given to certain artefacts from the site are shown thus: <100>. While it is not usual MoLAS practice to assign a numbered period solely to unstratified artefacts, we have done so for this site, as such material forms important evidence for prehistoric activity.
The graphical conventions used on the period plans in this report are shown in Fig 4.

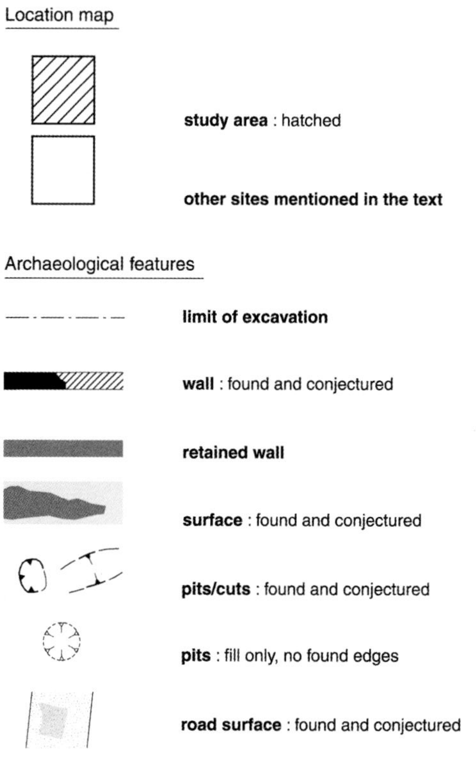

Fig 4 Graphical conventions used in this report

The archaeological sequence is expressed in terms of periods and land use. The periods are unique to the evidence from the site, and are based on a combination of artefactual dating and major stratigraphic development of the site. This report employs Building, Open Area, Road and Structure numbers (sometimes abbreviated to B, OA, R and S) collectively known as 'land uses'. These are, in general, numbered sequentially through the excavated sequence, from the earlier features to the later, and describe the history of the land use recorded on the site. They were derived during analysis of the site sequence, and form part of the database in the site archive. Features seen in both the 1954 and the 1996–9 fieldwork have been integrated into a single sequence of land uses; land-use numbers starting with 100 were seen only in the 1954 watching brief. The land-use text and accompanying drawings showing development over time are, of course, an interpretation of the findings as excavated, and do not necessarily describe the complete original structural history of the site, nor the only 'correct' way of presenting it. It should be noted that the 'Open Areas' are land uses, while 'area' denotes one of the areas of excavation into which the site was divided during fieldwork (see Fig 3).

2

The archaeological sequence

2.1 Natural geology and topography

Open Area 1: natural geology

During the excavation, only six observations were made of the Second Thames Terrace gravels, too few to reconstruct the original contours of the site in detail. They do, however, exhibit an overall slope down from north to south of 10.85m to 10.38m OD, and from west to east of 10.52m to 10.38m OD. These reflect the slopes down to the Thames and Walbrook, respectively (see 1.2 above).

The surviving surface of the brickearth was truncated at most, if not all, of the points where it was observed. The heights do, however, suggest a gentle slope from 11.55m OD in the north and west, down to 11.39m OD, or possibly 11.01m OD, in the south-east. It is likely that these levels reflect varying degrees of truncation, although the slope from west to east is similar to that of the underlying gravels.

2.2 Period 1: Middle Bronze Age occupation in the surrounding area (late 2nd millennium BC)

Residual Middle Bronze Age pottery

Louise Rayner

There was no *in situ* evidence for prehistoric activity on the site, but a layer of brickearth make-up for a Roman building (B2, period 2, see 2.3 below) produced an assemblage of 30 prehistoric sherds (Fig 5; Table 1), along with single examples of 2nd-century AD Roman pottery and ceramic

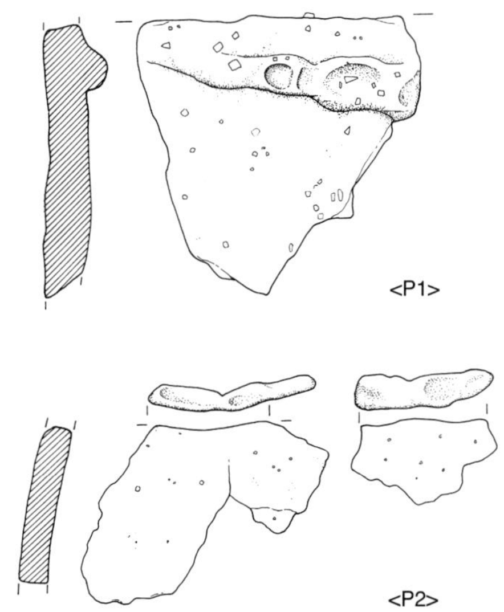

Fig 5 Middle Bronze Age pottery <P1> <P2>, recovered from a Roman deposit (1:2)

building material. These artefacts were concentrated in an area covering approximately 2.5 sq m. The sherds are in poor condition, highly fragmentary and abraded, and average sherd weight is less than 6g. Although there are some conjoining sherds, the condition of the material reinforces the interpretation that they were redeposited, rather than *in situ*.

Fabrics

The majority of the sherds are flint-tempered, with the exception of three sherds which have a soft, vesicular fabric (VOIDS). These sherds are very abraded and it is difficult to identify from the remaining voids in the fabric what the main inclusion was, although fine shell seems most likely. The flint-tempered sherds have been divided into two fabrics on basis of the density of the inclusions.

FLIN1 (FLMC): Hard, dense matrix with moderate crushed flint, coarse to very coarse in size (up to 4mm); very fine gold mica visible on the surfaces. Predominately oxidised surfaces with unoxidised core (see Fig 5).

FLIN2 (FLSC): Hard dense matrix with sparse coarse flint (generally 2mm or less, although rare larger inclusions are present up to 5mm). Unoxidised throughout (see Fig 5).

Table 1 Prehistoric pottery fabric groupings by count and weight

Fabric	Count	%	Weight (g)	%
FLIN1	24	80	150	89
FLIN2	3	10	14	8
VOIDS	3	10	5	3
Total	30		169	

Forms

Two joining body sherds have an applied finger-impressed cordon and come from a bucket urn of the southern British Deverel-Rimbury tradition. This decorative trait is seen on many other Deverel-Rimbury urns, including examples from Acton cemetery and Ashford Common, Sunbury (Barrett 1973, 114, fig 1 and 117, fig 4; Cotton 1993, 16, fig 10). There are two further sherds, which although not conjoining are likely to be from the same vessel. These appear to have a plain applied cordon and may come from a second large urn. An urn with a similar cordon was also found at the Acton cemetery (Barrett 1973, fig 117 no. 3).

The other feature sherds are simple rounded rims. Two of these join and are from a smaller urn of globular shape. The exterior surface is unburnished and there is no decoration on the surviving fragments; contraction cracks are visible. Although the fabric of this vessel is also flint-tempered, the inclusions are sparse and generally finer than those used for the bucket urns. The wall thickness is also thinner at *c* 7mm. Frequently Deverel-Rimbury globular urns have burnished surfaces and/or incised decoration, as well as bosses and perforations that are also found on bucket urns. However, plain examples are known and the variety that occurs in the fabrics may allow this vessel to be considered a globular urn.

The other rim fragment is similar, although it is not conjoining. The exterior surface is very damaged so the angle of the vessel wall cannot be discerned. Whether this is the same or a further vessel, the wall thickness (*c* 7mm) and fabric suggest it is likely to come from a relatively small urn, possibly globular, rather than a large bucket urn.

Catalogue

<P1> Body sherd with applied finger-impressed cordon from Deverel-Rimbury bucket urn (FLIN1)
<P2> Rim and shoulder from possible globular urn (FLIN2)

Residual flintwork

Jonathan Cotton

Three residual struck flints were also recovered from early Roman features in Open Area 9 (period 3, see 2.4 below), but were not associated with the Middle Bronze Age pottery. They may well have been brought to the site from a different location to the pottery. These are a bladelet, a secondary flake with wide striking platform, and a shattered fragment of a secondary flake. None of the pieces can be closely dated, but they could be of Neolithic or Bronze Age date.

Period discussion

Although finds of Deverel-Rimbury pottery are not unknown from central London, they generally consist of only a few sherds, mainly from residual contexts. Where diagnostic, the sherds are inevitably from the larger bucket urns. Recently, rim sherds from a bucket urn were recovered from Wood Street, London (Rayner in prep) and a few examples are known from Southwark, at St Thomas Street and Bermondsey Abbey (Sidell et al in prep) and from Westminster at Cromwell Green and Westminster Hall (Thomas et al in prep).

If the identification of the globular urn is accepted then it represents the only known example from the central London area. In the Thames Valley, Deverel-Rimbury globular urns are generally more common among settlement material, with a paucity of vessels from cremations or cemeteries. Of the seven surviving urns from Acton all are large bucket urns, and of the 30 urns from Ashford Common, only two are globular (Cotton 1993, 18). Other globular urns have been recovered from domestic contexts in the area to the west of London at Staines, Sipson and possibly Osterley (Cotton 1993, 16; Cotton 1981, 20, fig 1 no. 5), and at Wall Garden Farm and more recent excavations on the gravel terraces at Heathrow (MoLAS 1997).

The presence of both bucket and globular urns, therefore,

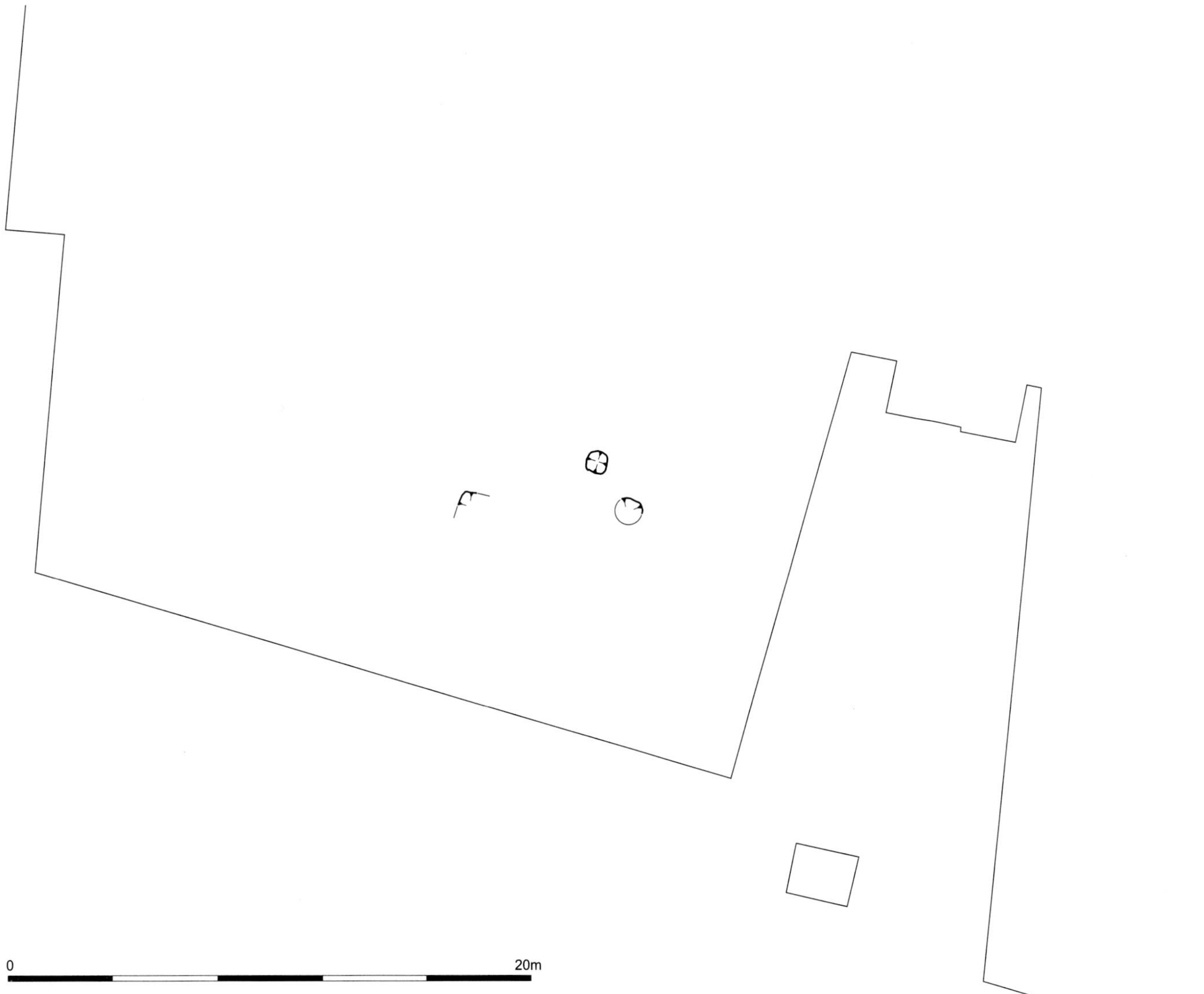

Fig 6 Plan of Roman quarrying, period 2

may indicate that this assemblage is more likely to derive from occupation activity, rather than being redeposited cremation vessels. As redeposited material, the assemblage cannot be taken as direct evidence for activity on this site. However, the brickearth and incorporated pottery is unlikely to have been brought over a long distance, so the activity was probably in the general vicinity of the site. Assuming that this was the case, the material provides further evidence of Middle Bronze Age activity in central London, a period which is generally less well represented than the later Bronze Age.

2.3 Period 2: Roman quarrying and the first timber buildings, *c* AD 50–70

A phase of quarrying of the natural brickearth and gravels forms the first activity after the Roman conquest in AD 43 (see Fig 6), and was probably contemporary with the first three buildings, and yards or alleys with gravel surfaces (see Fig 8).

Open Area 2: quarrying

The first *in situ* evidence for activity on the site were a number of cut features, most or all of which were probably quarry pits, forming Open Area 2 (Fig 6). The majority were backfilled with dirty brickearth, but those on the eastern side of the site had fills of distinctive greenish-brown sandy silt, and may have been either cesspits, or quarry pits backfilled with cessy material. The pits produced a few fragments of ox, sheep and pig bones with a single fragment of chicken; all material from adult animals. Given the extensive truncation from later activity on this site, it is not possible to draw any meaningful conclusions from the apparent clustering of the quarry pits.

This activity might have started as early as AD 50 or 55, although a minority of the pits must date to after AD 60.

A considerable quantity of ceramic roofing tile and brick

was dumped in the backfills of the quarry pits, and presumably represents destruction debris from buildings in the surrounding area. More unusual items include a fragment of box flue (fabric 2454) with knife-scored lattice keying, which must have come from a building with a hypocaust heating system, and a fragment of Purbeck marble from Dorset. The latter comprises a thin 15mm slab, which is smoothed flat on one side, but slightly less flat on the other (Fig 7). The less regular side has the remains of two shallow grooves, which perhaps acted as keying. This stone may have been used as wall inlay or as paving, although there are no other examples known from London with grooved bases.

The pits on the eastern side of the site produced fragments of glass vessels, largely finer tablewares, including three

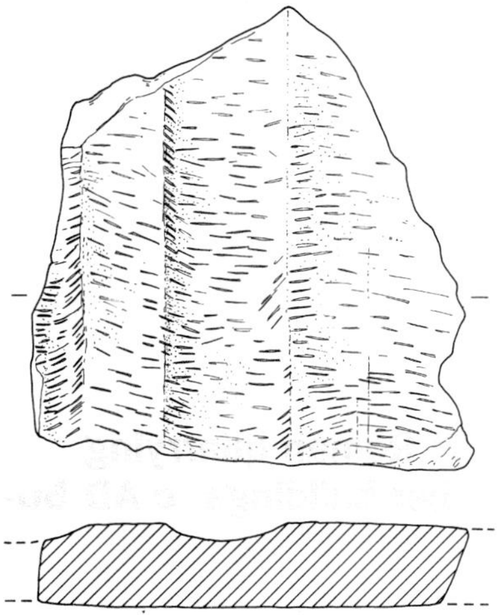

Fig 7 Fragment of Purbeck marble slab <213>, perhaps wall inlay or paving, recovered from the backfill of a quarry pit in Open Area 2 (1:2)

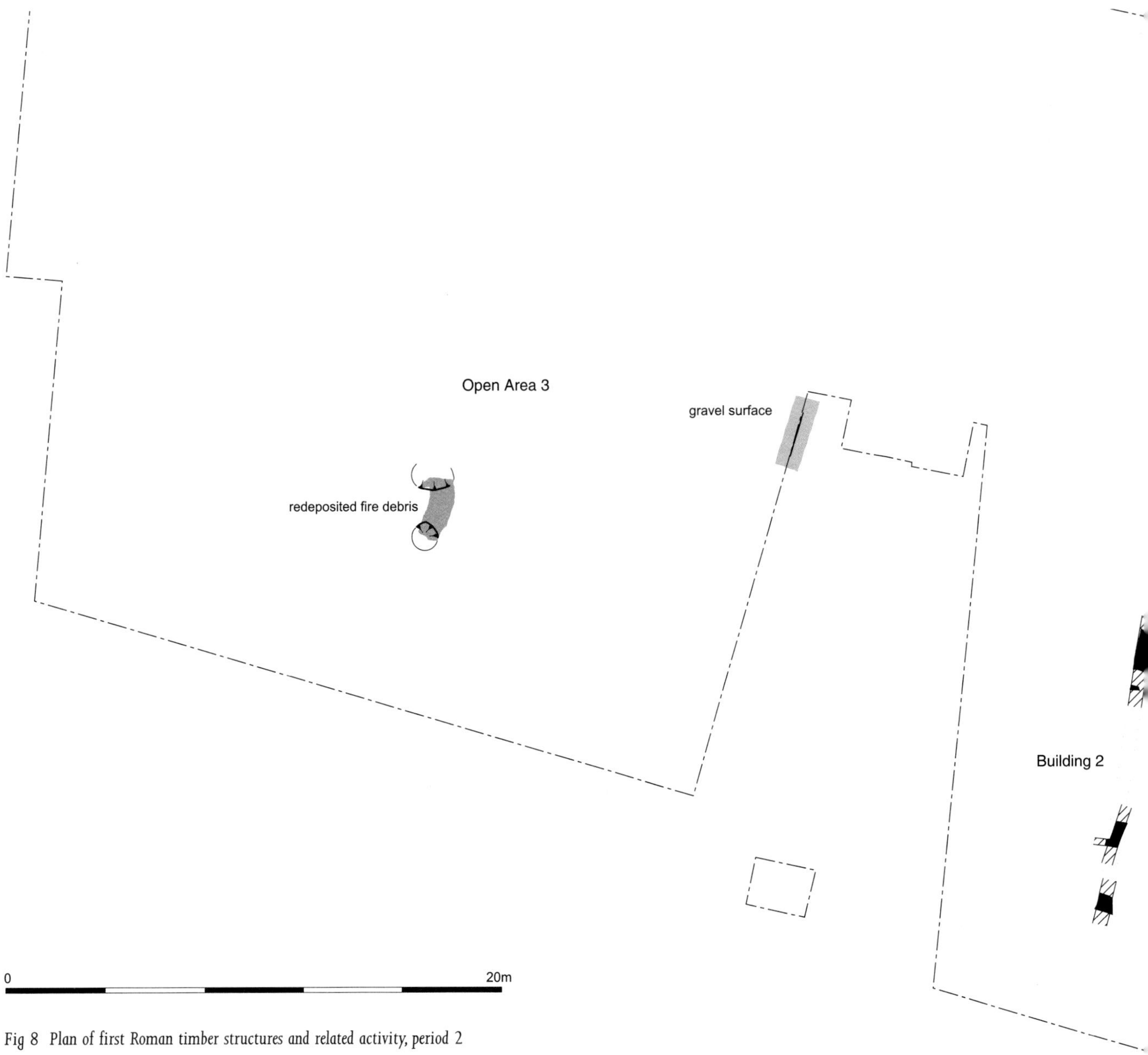

Fig 8 Plan of first Roman timber structures and related activity, period 2

fragments of the same dark blue bowl, <119>, <142> and <172>. Other finds include small fragments of a very corroded copper-alloy bow brooch, and a copper-alloy coin <27>, an irregular of Claudius I (AD 45–65).

Open Area 3: redeposited fire debris; and Open Area 4: pits

In Open Area 3 the backfilled quarry pits were sealed by redeposited brickearth make-up, c 0.4m deep, and there was a suggestion of a gravel yard or alley surface in the north-eastern corner (Fig 8). The make-up was overlain by redeposited fire debris, which also filled two pits, consisting of burnt daub, mudbrick and roof tile. The quantities of fire debris are sufficiently small to have been introduced from outside the site, but might, perhaps, indicate the presence of a mudbrick-and-daub building with a tiled roof, for which there is no other evidence.

A layer of redeposited brickearth make-up, c 0.4m deep, was laid down in Open Area 4. This was cut by three pits, one of which may have been formed by tree roots. These produced only a few fragments of chicken, sheep or goat, and pig bone.

Buildings 1–3: beam-slot foundations

Make-up was laid down, up to 0.5m deep, in preparation for Building 1, which was represented by beam slots. The north–south aligned beam slot had been backfilled with debris containing frequent charcoal, but there was no evidence for the timber itself, which had presumably been removed for reuse elsewhere. A second element met this on the eastern side, and might have formed an internal division. The backfills of the beam slots contained a small quantity of ceramic roofing tile, possibly from the roof of the structure, and a fragment of brick, perhaps from a hearth or pathway. A few small fragments of red and plain white plaster suggest that it had decorated walls.

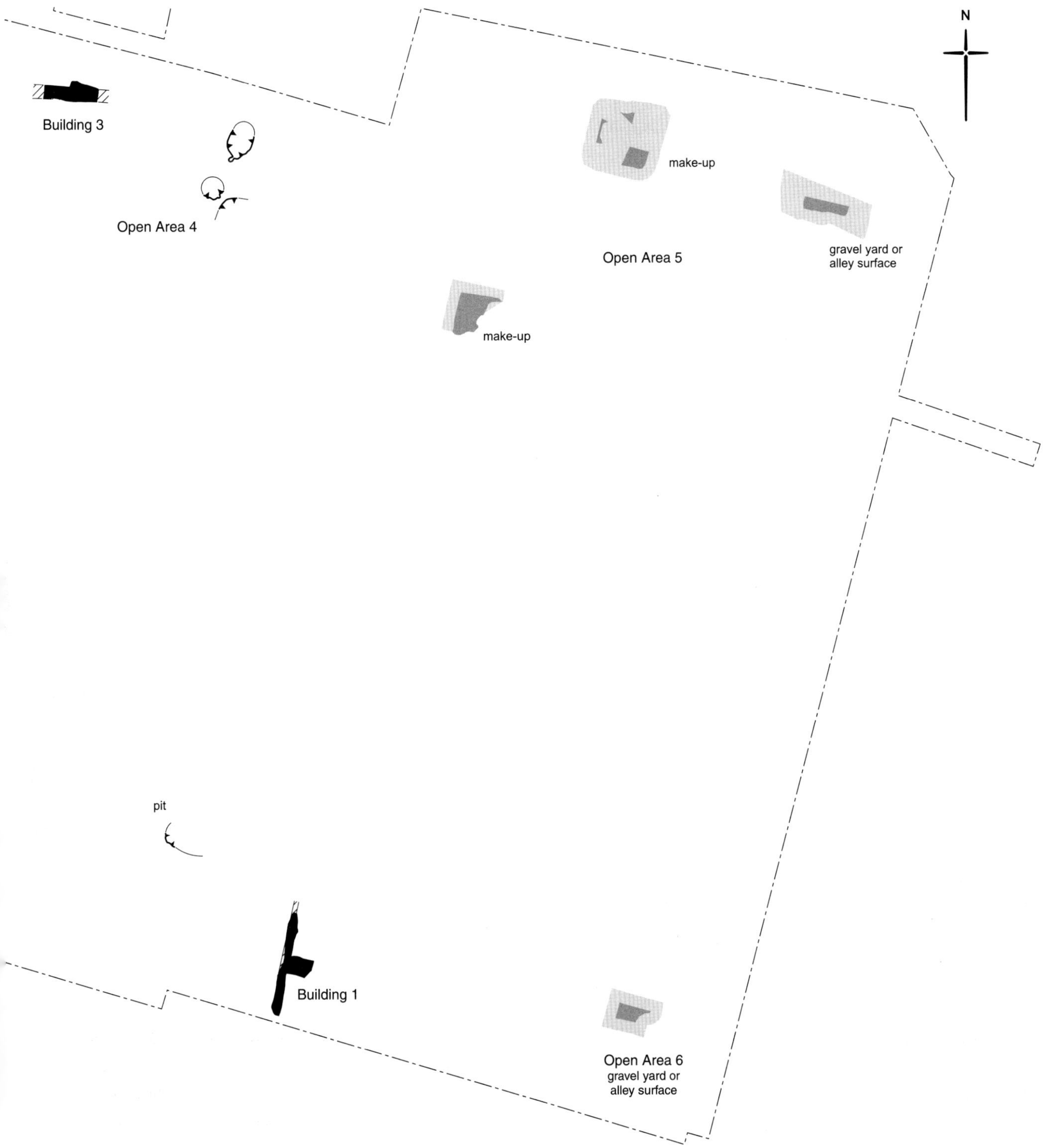

Redeposited brickearth, 0.5m deep, was laid as make-up in advance of the construction of Building 2, the remains of which consisted of a number of truncated sections of beam slots. They appear to have been from two or more buildings, although given the fragmentary nature of the remains it is possible that they actually formed one structure, aligned north–south. The make-up contained residual Middle Bronze Age pottery (see 2.2 above), as well as single fragments of Roman pottery and tile.

Building 3 was a single beam slot aligned east–west, forming part of a building or other structure.

Open Areas 5 and 6: make-up overlain by gravel surfaces

Open Area 5 was make-up layers, which survived up to 0.3m deep, overlain at one point by the remains of a gravel surface. Open Area 6 was redeposited brickearth make-up, up to 0.45m deep, sealed by a gravel surface some 0.30m deep. These two surfaces could have been alley or yard surfaces.

Table 2 Selected dating evidence, period 2 (c AD 50–70)

Land use	Context	Evidence	Description	Sherds	Date range
B1	[1594]	pottery	GROG 2; ?HWB 4F; SAMLG	6	60–100
B1	[1586]	pottery	FMIC; LYON 3 RCD1; SAMLG 4DR29 DEC, 4RT12, 6DR27	31	50–70
OA2	[1491]	pottery	FMIC 3C NCD; GAUL1 8G5; HWB 4F NCD WL; OXID 4F HPOF unusual fabric, interior with red-painted surface; large joining sherds with good examples of vessel types	21	60–100
OA2	[1457]	pottery	CAT 8DR2–4; ERMS; ERSB 2; HOO; LYON 6H ROD (Greene type 10; RCD1 internally); RHOD 8	28	50–70
OA2	[1358]	pottery	BAETE 8DR20PW7; COAR (large quartz inclusions); ECCW 2 HPRF; ERMS 2B; FMIC 3C; GAUL1 8G; HOO; HWB 2A; HWBR 5; OXID ?3 (long neck and simple rim), 6 (sparse VRW-like fabric; thin-walled cup ?6A; square rim); RDBK 3 BRD; SAMLG 4 ROD (unusual rim not typical DR29), 4DR29 DEC, 4RT12; 6 complete stamp; TN 5J (Camulodunum form 16); VRW 81J (collared rim)	111	50–80
OA2	[1223]	pottery	RDBK 3B BDD; SAMLG 4DR29 ROD	20	55–100
OA2	[1447]	coin	Irregular of Claudius I <27>		45–65
OA4	[936]	pottery	FMIC 3 NCD (NCD = XXX bordered by incised lines); OXID 2 HPRF (fabric similar to LOXI; unusual vessel with crude large hole in side)	42	50–120
OA6	[432]	pottery	VRW 81J	11	50–100

Period discussion

As Buildings 2 and 3 did not overlie quarry pits, it seems likely that at least some of the quarrying was contemporary with the occupation of those buildings, as opposed to separate phases of quarrying and construction. Building 1 might represent a later phase of construction within this period. While most of the quarrying, and Buildings 2 and 3, could date from as early as AD 50 or 55 (Table 2), the pits which preceded Building 1 contained material which postdates AD 60, reinforcing this suggestion. None of this activity, however, can definitely be said to have taken place before AD 60, and consideration of the pottery assemblage as a whole reinforces the suggestion that quarrying and occupation may not have commenced until after that date.

There was no evidence for organised land division before the first construction, such as marker posts or enclosure ditches. The parallel alignments of Buildings 1 and 2, however, suggest that the buildings respected either regular plots of land, or a topographical feature, such as a road or the hill slope. It may be coincidence, but a line connecting the gravel surfaces in Open Areas 5 and 6 (see Fig 8) can be connected to form an alignment that is parallel to that of Building 1, and also to Building 100 in the earlier part of period 3 (see Fig 9). They may have been parts of a gravel alley, that postdated the quarrying in Open Area 2, but which was contemporary with the later construction in period 2, and lasted into period 3.

The burnt mudbrick in Open Area 3 may indicate a fourth building, but could have been introduced from outside the site. Given the extensive truncation, occupation may well have been considerably more intensive than is suggested by the excavated evidence. This observation holds true for all of the periods of occupation on the site.

The small assemblages of animal bone recovered from the quarry pits of Open Area 2 and the make-up of Open Area 4 derived from small numbers of adult chicken, ox, sheep or goat, sheep and pig fragments, suggesting consumption of chicken, beef, mutton and pork.

2.4 Period 3: timber and first masonry buildings, *c* AD 70–140

Period 3 saw extensive reconstruction of the buildings in the eastern half of the site (Fig 9), and Buildings 1 and 2 appear to be retained from period 2. Building 3 was replaced by Buildings 4 and 5. Building 8 was constructed, and subsequently replaced by another timber structure, Building 9. The first masonry building, Building 100, was constructed on the eastern margin of the site, but was soon replaced by the more extensive Building 10 (see Fig 12). There was evidence for gravel-surfaced yards between buildings, while rubbish pits were dug elsewhere.

Building 4: robbed foundation

Building 4 replaced Building 3, and was represented by a robbed foundation trench, 0.72m wide and at least 0.49m deep. A few flint nodules, measuring up to 0.30m, survived at the base of the backfill, which may be the remnants of a flint bedding for a wall of either brickearth, timber or possibly masonry.

Building 5: timber-shuttered wall

The remains of Building 5 consisted of a construction trench 1.22m wide, containing a series of rectangular stakeholes along each of the edges, which may have held up shuttering for a substantial brickearth wall. The stakeholes and the lower 70mm

Fig 9 Plan of the earlier structures in period 3, including the first Roman masonry building (B100)

of the feature were filled with a clay silt, overlain by compacted sandy gravel, which may have been bedding for a baseplate or sill beam, later robbed. The clay silt contained a natural green-blue glass cylindrical bead <158>.

This would appear to be the foundation trench for a substantial timber-framed or shuttered wall, perhaps of brickearth construction. The gravel may have been a bedding layer for the superstructure. There is no direct parallel for this type of construction from London, and it is possible that it was a drain.

If the building extended to the west of the wall, then its extent would be incompatible with Building 4. Even if Building 5 extended to the east of the wall, the close proximity, and differing orientations, of the two buildings would also suggest that they were not contemporary (see Fig 9). It is not possible, however, to determine the order in which they were constructed.

To the east of the wall, a number of postholes had been constructed, probably forming more than one structure. Elements of the post settings may have been a disturbed beam slot. It is possible to reconstruct an alignment from the beam slot and some of the postholes, which lay at 90° to the timber-shuttered foundation. This could have been an internal partition within Building 5, with other postholes belonging to other internal structures. Alternatively, the posts could have formed parts of structures outside the building.

Open Area 9: boundary ditch, rubbish and cesspits

Some of the eastern part of the site seems to have been occupied by a scattering of pits, probably for rubbish and cess disposal. One pit produced a small fragment of bottle glass <91>, dating to the late 1st to 2nd centuries AD. A substantial ditch, 1.52m wide and 0.94m deep, appears to have been a major drainage, and perhaps boundary, ditch (Fig 10). Its primary cut lay parallel to Building 100 (see below), and contained pottery dated to AD 70–80. The first recut changed the alignment slightly to become parallel with Building 10; this event is undated, but a later recut contained pottery dated to AD 100–60.

Fig 10 View of the ditch in Open Area 9, from the south

Buildings 8 and 9: beam-slot and post-built structures

Building 8 consisted of robbed beam slots, 0.58m wide, and postholes, forming part of a building based on timber baseplates or beams, which could have been two separate structures (Fig 11). A short length of beam slot to the west of the main alignment was probably part of a relatively substantial internal wall. The postholes appeared to belong to either internal partitions or to external structures, to the east of the main wall. Building 8 produced a few fragments of adult ox, sheep or goat, and pig bone.

Fig 11 View of beam slot and postholes from timber Buildings 8 and 9, from the north (0.5m scale)

Building 8 was replaced by Building 9, which appeared to be another building with timber sill beams at least 0.50m wide, and sharing the same orientation as Building 8 (see Fig 12). This was represented by a beam slot which lay immediately to the west of the main alignment of the earlier building, with a post pad of rough lumps of Kentish rag in the base. This might represent either a separate structure from Building 8, or substantial repairs or rebuilding of that structure. The backfill of the beam slot produced a fragment of a small glass jar with a wide, overhanging rim, <114>, possibly from a cosmetic or unguent jar.

Building 100: masonry building with brickearth floors

Building 100 was recorded in 1954, and appears to have been the western side of the first substantial masonry building on the site, defining a room or rooms *c* 6.0m across. It was constructed of Kentish rag with two tile bonding courses, and an offset foundation, and was faced with wall plaster on the eastern side. The masonry walls survived to a height of 0.85m above the footing, suggesting an all-stone construction, rather than brickearth or timber above dwarf stone walls (Shepherd 1986, fig 8 cf fig 6). A burnt 'clay' (?brickearth) floor provided evidence of a fire, after which the building continued in use, with a new 'clay' floor being laid over a *c* 0.30m deep bed of Kentish rag chippings (Shepherd 1986, 135, figs 8 and 10, 'Building 4').

The walls cut a pit containing pottery dated to AD 55–80 in Open Area 2, and this building was probably constructed *c* AD 70–80, and demolished by *c* AD 100. The wall was partly cut away to accommodate a stone-lined drain, but the date at which this occurred cannot be determined. The drain may well postdate Building 100, as a similar drain appeared to be associated with the later Building 10 (see below).

Building 10: extensive masonry building

Greenish cessy deposits in area C2 probably represent levelling of the earlier cesspits in advance of new construction. The

Fig 12 Plan of later structures in period 3: Building 10 which replaced Building 100; Building 9 replacing Building 8; Open Area 10; and also the recutting of the ditch in Open Area 9

make-up produced <115>, part of a glass pillar-moulded bowl, dating to the mid to late 1st century, and part of a corroded copper-alloy hairpin <25> with a plain globular head.

Building 10 encroached further on Open Area 9, and replaced Building 100 (Fig 12). Different walls from the building, constructed of Kentish rag, were seen in the recent fieldwork and the 1954 watching brief (Shepherd 1986, 138–9, figs 11 and 12, 'Building 10', but note that the 'plain mosaic' actually belongs to Building 21). The measurements of these walls will be described in more detail than others in this report, as they appear to vary with their function. The northern wall was 0.70m wide, with a foundation offset by 0.12m on the southern side (Fig 13). The other east–west walls were 0.53m wide, offset by *c* 0.11m to both the north

Fig 13 View of the northern wall of Building 10, from the south-west. The earlier deposits into which the foundations had been cut have been removed out of sequence, showing the better-quality masonry above Roman ground level, and the poorer-quality work of the offset foundation

and south. Two short lengths of wall, 0.45m wide, formed the remnants of an internal dividing wall.

These variations in width and offsets suggest that the northern wall was external, separated by a corridor *c* 2.0m wide, designated room A, from two rooms, which together measured 9.6m by more than 11.2m (rooms B and C). There was probably another external wall to the south of rooms B and C, that lay outside the limits of excavation or was truncated by later activity. If so, an isolated area of *opus signinum* floor to the south of room C probably belonged to a fourth room: room D.

Part, at least, of room C had mortar floors, which sealed the stumps of the walls of Building 100. The southern part of this room probably had a mosaic floor, although it is possible that this belonged to Building 21 (see 2.6 below). This would suggest that 'room C' actually formed two or more rooms separated by partition walls which either did not survive or lay outside the areas of excavation. One of the two sections of poor-quality mosaic was laid in a chequer-board pattern of green and white squares (Fig 14). Between the latter and the southern surviving wall of room C lay an area of coarse white tesserae, probably from a border of the mosaic.

A drain passed through the southern wall of Building 10, and was constructed of 0.4m wide Kentish rag walls, rendered with plaster, and a tile base. It is not possible to determine whether this was part of the original structure, or a later addition.

The full extent of this building cannot be determined: no remains of it were recorded on the eastern side of Bread Street at Watling House in 1954 (see Fig 46; Shepherd 1986, fig 3).

Fig 14 View of the green and white chequered mosaic observed in the 1954 watching brief; it may have belonged to either Building 10 or 21 (Guildhall Museum)

Table 3 Selected dating evidence, period 3 (c AD 70–140)

Land use	Context	Evidence	Description	Sherds	Date range
B4	[973]	pottery	HWC	5	70–100
B5	[787]	pottery	AHSU 9A; OXID 9A; SAMLG 6DR33, 6 <175> illegible stamp	9	70–100
B10	[1253]	pottery	AHSU 2A; BHWS; EGGS; ERMS 5A; ERSB 2; FLIN; GAUL2 8; HOO; HWB; OXID 1A; RDBK 3 BDD; SAMLG 4DR29 ROD; SAND 9A; only EGGS has earliest date of AD 70	65	70–80
B10	[1472]	pottery	ERMS 2; SAMLG 6DR27; SAND 9A, 2D BUD, fabric similar to ERSB; VRW 1A	12	60–100
OA9	[1079]	pottery	HWC 2E BUD	8	100–60
OA9	[1260]	pottery	HWC 4F	3	70–160

The ditch in Open Area 9 (see above) appeared to be aligned parallel to the north–south dividing wall of Building 10 (see Fig 12). It might have marked or reflected a boundary which continued south past the western side of the building. If so, this would suggest that room B was no more than 5.5m in width.

The date at which Building 100 was demolished and Building 10 constructed is difficult to determine; it was possibly *c* AD 100, and could have been in the early 2nd century, but certainly no earlier than AD 70 (Table 3).

Building 16: masonry wall with buttress

A Kentish rag wall, *c* 0.5m in width, was oriented approximately north–south and was associated with a mortar floor. It may have had a buttress added, extending *c* 1.4m from the western side of the wall. This may, therefore, have been the western wall of a building extending further to the east beneath modern Bread Street. Its orientation and date are unclear, and it has been assigned to this period by comparison with Building 10, to which buttresses were also added, and whose walls were also razed to ground level and sealed by the floors of Building 21 (see 2.6 below; 2.5 for buttresses).

Open Area 7: gravel yard surface

Brickearth make-up was laid in preparation for a gravel surface. While it is possible that this was an alleyway between buildings, it is probable that this was part of a more extensive yard surface.

Open Areas 8 and 10: make-up

Open Area 8 was represented by make-up overlain by orange brickearth, Open Area 10, which may also have been deposited as make-up, or possibly as the floors of various buildings, including Building 16 (see above).

Period discussion

Period 3 saw the first appearance of masonry buildings on the site, supplementing, but not wholly supplanting, the timber structures. The two building techniques coexisted on the site until the end of Roman occupation. Open Area 9 was increasingly encroached upon during period 3 by the construction of Buildings 8, 9, 100 and 10. Open Area 9 had probably disappeared, or been reduced to alleys and yards between the buildings, by the end of the period. The masonry buildings and later activities may have truncated the remains of any timber buildings which preceded Buildings 100 and 10, although one of the pits in Open Area 9, which was cut by Building 10, suggests that the latter was constructed partially on open ground.

Buildings 1 and 2 may well have continued in use from the preceding period, although it might be that period 3 activity has been lost to truncation in areas D1 and D2, and they share an orientation with Buildings 8, 9 and 100. There is a continuity of alignments, at least in the south-eastern quarter of the site, from period 2, until the construction of Building 10.

With the construction of Building 10 there is a slight, but notable, change of alignment, which is shared by Building 5, and in the recutting of the ditch in Open Area 9. There is no evidence for any event which might have prompted this change (but see 3.1 below), which is not closely dated, but probably occurred towards the end of the 1st century AD.

The alignment of Building 4 corresponds approximately to that of Building 2, and may, therefore, have been part of an earlier phase of construction which included Buildings 1, 8, 9 and 100. As Buildings 4 and 5 were probably not contemporary (see 'Building 5' above), this suggests that Building 5 replaced Building 4.

Period 3 commences *c* AD 70–80. The majority of the pottery has a *terminus ante quem* (TAQ) of AD 100, but the remainder could have been made as late as AD 160. Allowing that some of the earlier pottery could be residual, it is probable that this period ends at a point within the first half of the 2nd century, with some buildings going out of use shortly after AD 100. Building 10, as discussed above, was probably constructed by AD 100, and the latest recut of the ditch in Open Area 9 postdates AD 100, demonstrating later activity within this period.

The animal bone assemblage from period 3 consists of scattered fragments of chicken, ox, sheep or goat, and pig. It is similar to that from period 2, with the exception of dog bones from the make-up for Building 10, which provide some evidence for the disposal of domestic animals that had not been consumed.

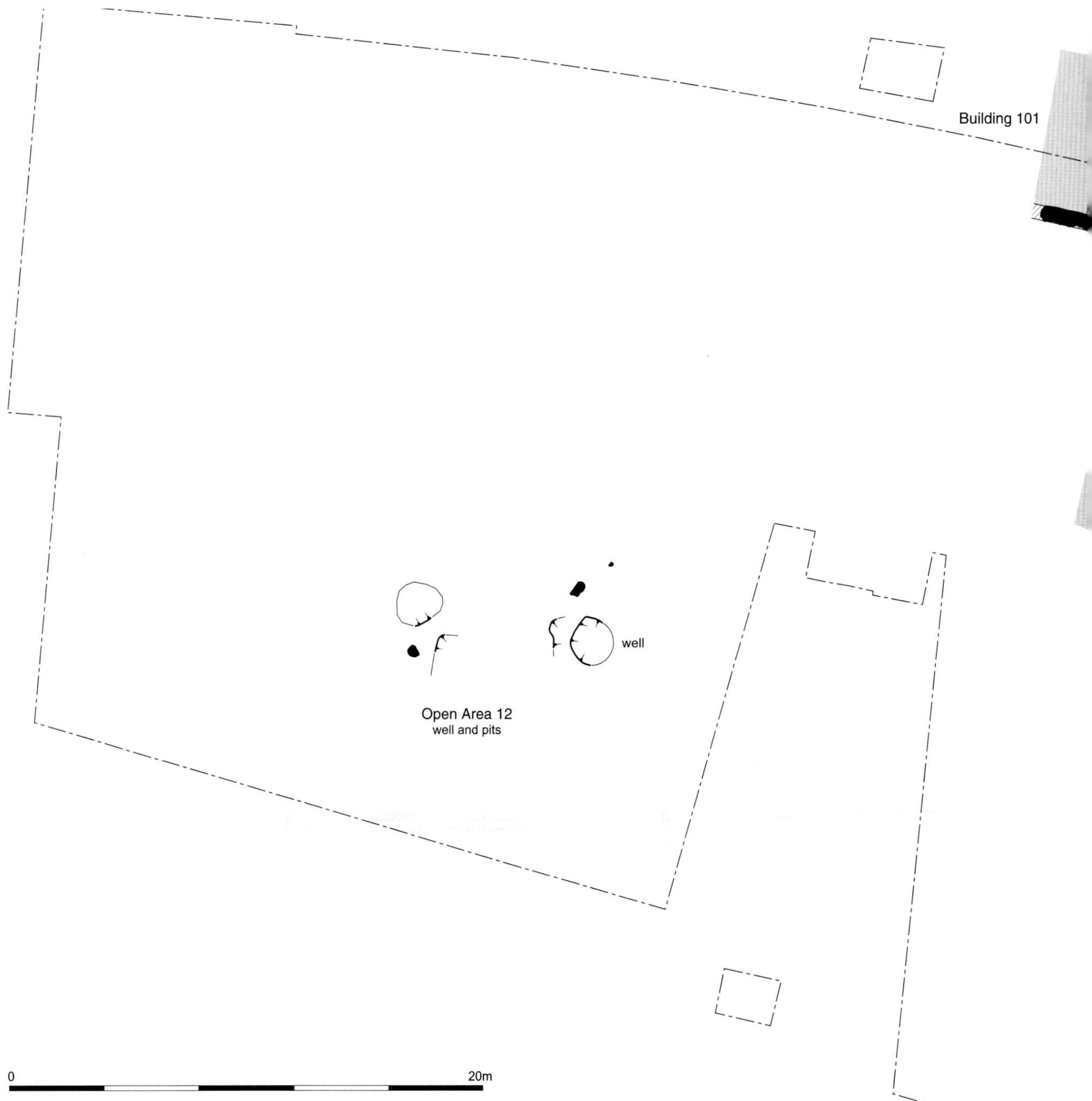

Fig 15 Plan of period 4 structures, showing extensive construction on two differing alignments, including the addition of buttresses to Building 10, and Open Area 100 separating Buildings 10 and 17

Table 4 Selected dating evidence, period 4 (c *AD* 140–250)

Land use	Context	Evidence	Description	Sherds	Date range
B7	[1146]	pottery	BB2 2F, 4H AL; HWC 2E BUD, 3 BDD; KOLN 3 RCD2; RWS 1B7–9; SAMCG 4DR37, 6DR33; VRW 9C	50	140–60
B10	[1424]	building material	2459B, 2815, 3060, 3500: forming part of buttress		140–250
B13	[1583]	building material	2454		140–250
B15	[1336]	pottery	BBS 2F	4	120–250
OA12	[391]	building material	2459B, 2815		140–250
OA13	[775]	pottery	HWC 2E BUD, 3F4 BDD	21	100–60
OA13	[739]	pottery	?BB1 4 SL (?4H); BB2 4H AL; ?BB2F 4/5 AL; KOLN RCD2; SAMCG 6DR33 <174> stamp C.R.CIRO.OFI; SAMLG 4DR37 DEC; VRW 7HOF, 'late' 7HOF	24	140–200

2.5 Period 4: more intensive construction, *c* AD 140–250

Period 4 includes extensive evidence for construction across all of the areas of excavation, except those truncated by later activity (Fig 15). Buttresses were added to Building 10, and ten new buildings were constructed (Table 4).

Addition of buttresses to Building 10

At some point after AD 140, two buttresses were built on to the northern wall of Building 10, apparently in response to subsidence, as the foundations were found leaning at a small, but noticeable, angle to the vertical. The western and eastern buttresses were 2.14m and 1.30m wide, respectively, and both extended 1.60m from the wall. They were situated some 2.3m apart; if there had been other buttresses spaced similarly, then they would have been truncated or outside the area of excavation. No other external walls of this building were seen, so it is not known whether buttresses were added to other faces of the structure.

Building 6: masonry foundation and robber trench

Building 6 was represented by a heavily truncated length of Kentish rag, tile, and chalk foundation or wall, 0.6m wide, and a robber trench which probably contained a wall of similar width, although it was 1.30m wide at the top.

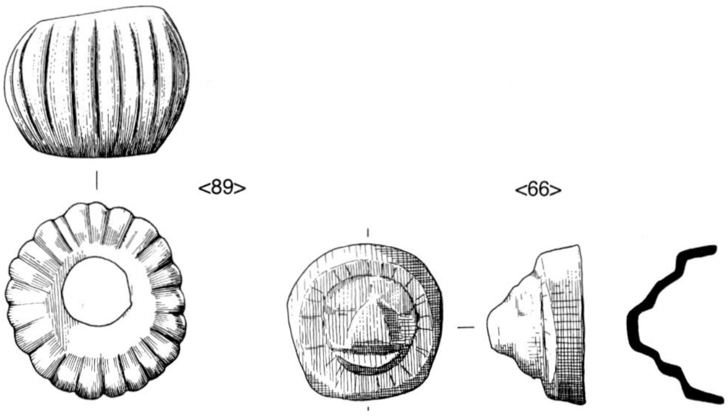

Fig 16 Dark turquoise glass melon bead <89>, and copper-alloy lionhead mount dating to the 1st century AD <66>, from make-up layers in Open Area 13 (1:1)

Building 7: timber-framed walls

It is difficult to determine precisely how these walls were constructed, and whether they represent one or two buildings in the same position. Building 7 appeared to have two substantial timber-framed walls, *c* 1.5m in width, that to the east incorporating posts with an odd arrangement of stakes beneath. Either the posts replaced groups of stakes, or the stakes supported the posts. It is possible that the two walls were from different structures with the same orientation, although the widths were similar, and both seem to have been robbed or disturbed after AD 350.

Open Area 13 and Building 11: stone and gravel foundation

Make-up was laid in preparation for an unusual foundation, consisting of a 0.79m wide trench with a single layer of ragstone rubble rammed into the base, and then levelled over with layers of gravel. This may have been the footing for a substantial wall, perhaps timber-framed. The make-up produced a dark turquoise glass melon bead <89> and a copper-alloy lionhead mount <66> (Fig 16).

Open Area 14 and Building 12: beam-slot structure and fire debris

Make-up containing fire debris was laid in advance of the construction of Building 12, and may indicate the presence of an earlier building for which no other evidence survived. A thin layer of gravel may have been part of the make-up or an external surface. The largest element was a beam slot, 0.65m wide, containing the heavily decayed remnants of a beam 0.15m in width and 0.13m high, with the remnants of Kentish rag packing on either side.

To the north a feature of near identical construction was recorded, although it seemed misaligned with that to the south, and of greater width, suggesting the possibility that they lay on either side of a wall at right angles to them. A third beam slot, heavily truncated, lay parallel with the others. These may have been elements of one or more buildings.

Buildings 101 and 13: masonry walls

Building 101 consisted of two short lengths of Kentish rag walling, possibly from separate structures, the northern section having one tile bonding course, and the southern wall two. The construction materials contrast with those from other buildings in the vicinity: Buildings 7, 11 and 12.

Building 13 consisted of five sections of Kentish rag wall sharing the same alignment. It is highly likely that they represent more than one building, as they were of differing widths. The northernmost section returned to the west, suggesting that it represents the eastern side of a building, or an internal partition. The central section of the five, however, had remnants of wall plaster on its eastern face. To the east of this, two other sections of wall, with similar orientations and widths, might belong to Building 13 or 10.

Building 14: masonry wall; Building 15: post pad; and Building 102: mortar floor and burning

Building 14 consisted of three sections of wall or foundation, that could have been parts of one or more buildings which continued the alignment of Building 13. All three had Kentish rag as their main material, but one section included flint and gravel, another chalk. It is possible that these were parts of much later buildings, reusing stone from Roman structures.

Building 15 replaced Building 9, and consisted of just a Kentish rag and tile post pad. If the alignment of Building 14 represents the eastern wall of a building, in the same manner as suggested for Building 13, then this post pad might have been part of an internal structure from the same building.

An area of 'coarse red tesserae' observed in 1954 may belong to Building 14/15. Another section from what was probably the same tessellated floor (monochrome mosaic) was found nearby in 1998, collapsed into a medieval cesspit. It had ended up vertically: a situation most unnatural for a floor (Fig 17). It consisted of a base of mortar mixed with gravel and ceramic building material fragments, 90mm thick, over which was a bed of sandy mortar 40mm deep. On to this the tesserae, 24–30mm sq, were set in white mortar. They had been made from tiles produced AD 140–300. The work had been fairly coarsely executed and, although it incorporates some dark grey tesserae, does not appear to be patterned. The size of the tesserae and the roughness of the work suggest that this floor was utilitarian rather than decorative.

The only evidence for Building 102 (not illustrated) was a mortar floor, overlain by a layer of burnt wood, suggesting that it was destroyed by fire. Building 102 might have been part of Building 14 or 15.

Fig 17 View of a section of tessellated floor that had collapsed into a medieval pit, and ended up resting vertically, from the south

Building 17: partially burnt masonry building; Buildings 18 and 19

Building 17 was formed from a number of sections of Kentish rag wall seen in 1954; in the 1999 watching brief two walls were observed in a corresponding location. The walls had been very heavily burned, oxidising both faces to depths of 100–230mm. The fire damage may have been localised, rather than part of a fire which resulted in the destruction of the whole building, explaining the absence of burning on the walls recorded in 1954.

The walls exhibited the same range of widths as those of Building 10 (see 2.4 above), and room A formed a similar corridor, or range of small rooms, to Building 10 room A. It is unclear whether Building 17 extended to the north or south of the corridor. The wall forming its northern side was 0.71m thick, and that to the south was 0.52m. Comparison with Building 10 suggests that the corridor formed the northern side of the building. A wall on the northern boundary of the site, however, parallel to the corridor, had its foundation offset to the south. It may have formed the northern wall of the building.

The north–south wall on the western side of Building 17 may have been external. If so, the ditch in Open Area 9 may have extended along the western side of Building 17.

Pottery recovered from the construction cut of one of the walls in 1954 would indicate that Building 17 was built after AD 200, but this could well have been later disturbance. If so, then this building may have been constructed at the same time as Building 10, *c* AD 100, whose alignment it shares.

A masonry wall or foundation, and a robber cut on a distinctive alignment, have been grouped as Building 18. They could well be elements of different structures, and might belong to later periods, as they appear incompatible with Buildings 10 and 17. The alignments may be the result of truncation or the limited area of these features that was exposed, thus their extents have not been conjectured in Fig 15.

The Kentish rag walls of Building 19 shared the alignment of the northern elements of Building 17. If they belonged to the same structure, then it would form a narrow building extending for some 25m. If they were separate buildings, they may have been laid on either side of a projection to the north of the ditch in Open Area 9.

Open Areas 11 and 100: gravel surfaces; Open Area 12: well and pits

The gravel yard or alley surface of Open Area 11 was laid over the construction cut on both sides of the western wall of Building 7, but not, apparently, across the line of the wall itself. Either this includes both internal and external gravel surfaces, or the surface postdates that building.

Open Area 100 was a 120mm deep rammed gravel surface, located between Buildings 10 and 17, part of either a yard or alleyway.

Make-up was laid down in Open Area 12, and a well and several pits were established. A large volume of mudbrick came from a pit in Open Area 12, where over 40 fragments were dumped, along with a number of heat-cracked roofing tiles and bricks. This may have been the remains of a kiln structure or hearth, or simply debris from a burnt-down building.

Period discussion

The buildings of period 4 exhibited two slightly differing alignments, which, allowing for the vagaries of locating the 1954 evidence, are divided between an eastern group consisting of Buildings 10, 17 and probably 19, and the remaining buildings to the west. The extensive masonry Buildings 10 and 17 lay on either side of a gravel courtyard or alley (OA100), contrasting with timber Buildings 7, 11 and 12. The extent of Building 10 suggests a building of moderate status, perhaps a large townhouse. The green and white chequered mosaic was of relatively poor quality compared with that from Watling Court (Perring and Roskams 1991, 88–90).

To the west, Buildings 7, 11 and 12 were more prosaic timber, earth or mudbrick constructions, although the widths of their foundation walls suggest fairly substantial structures.

The animal bone assemblage was a little larger than those from earlier periods, and exhibited similar characteristics to that from period 2.

Fig 18 Plan of period 5 Roman structures, showing the distinctive alignment of Building 20, and the extensive tessellated floors of Building 21

2.6 Period 5: later Roman redevelopment, *c* AD 250 to ? early 5th century

Buildings 10 and 16 were demolished and replaced by a building with extensive tessellated floors (Fig 18). Buildings 11 and 12 were replaced by a single building on a new and distinctive alignment. Pits in Open Areas 16 and 17 may be of Roman or later date (Fig 19).

Robbing of Building 7

Building 7 continued in use from the preceding period until some point after AD 350, when the walls were robbed or dismantled.

Open Area 15 and Building 20

After the robbing of Building 12, make-up was laid for a phase of activity for which there was no other evidence. Further make-up was later laid for Building 20.

Evidence for Building 20 consisted of lengths of masonry wall with a singular orientation, and an area of mortar floor which might have been associated (Fig 20). It is unclear whether these walls represent a single building, or two sharing the same orientation. Two small patches of off-white wall plaster, over a pink mortar rendering similar to *opus signinum*, survived on the southern wall of room A. This and the return of that wall to the south indicate that the wall formed an internal division, separating rooms A and B. A length of wall observed in 1954 might have formed the northern side of the building. The date at which this building was constructed is not clearly defined, but was probably *c* AD 200–50, or possibly later.

Any great extent of room B to the south of the surviving walls would appear to be incompatible with Building 7, especially if it included the area of mortar floor. Given the late date of the robbing of the latter building, this is puzzling, as it might indicate a date after AD 350 for the construction of Building 20. If, however, the mortar floor did not belong to Building 20, then room B might have formed a narrow room or corridor *c* 2m wide, that would not necessarily impinge on Building 7.

Building 21: tessellated floors

Building 21 room A

Buildings 10 and 16 were razed, and the buttresses of Building 10 were partially robbed after AD 250, dated by pottery from the backfill of one of the robber cuts (Table 5).

Curiously, there were no walls that could be clearly identified with the new building, but extensive plain red tessellated floors were laid over the stumps of the walls of the previous buildings. These were laid on a substantial series of bedding layers, consisting firstly of 100–150mm of Kentish rag rubble, consolidated with 80–160mm of a poor-quality concrete, consisting of equal proportions of fine flint gravel and off-white mortar. On this base was laid a bed of pink mortar, *opus signinum*, 20–30mm deep, on which the red tesserae were laid in and on a thin layer of fine white mortar or grouting, *c* 5mm deep. The tesserae, *c* 15mm sq, had been manufactured from tile that had been produced between AD 50 and 160. There was also one yellow cube, from tile produced between AD 50 and 80. The size and dating of the tesserae, as well as the composition of the base, differed noticeably from those of Building 14/15 (see 2.5 above).

Room A must originally have covered an area exceeding 10m x 15m, although this may actually have been divided by partitions. There was, however, no evidence of any wall dividing the 10m width on the southern side of this expanse. This implies a room of considerable size, and consequent status of the building's inhabitants.

Building 21 room B

A second tessellated floor sealed the razed wall of Building 16. Here the red tesserae were bordered with an off-white band of hard chalk tesserae, at least 0.18m wide; the former were constructed from tile produced in AD 50–160. One grey cube of Kentish rag was mixed in with the red; a difficult stone to cut accurately, its use as a tessera is very unusual in London. The tesserae had been laid on a very similar sequence of bedding layers to that of room A, with the exception that the *opus signinum* had been laid in two separate layers of slightly differing colour. This may simply represent the *opus signinum* having been laid in two sessions, or possibly a resurfacing of the tessellated floor. As the distinctive sequence of basal layers was the same as that for room A, it seems unlikely that this is a tessellated floor laid over an earlier plain *opus signinum* floor.

While the presence of the white border, and the slight differences in construction and materials, indicate that this formed a different room from room A, there is no indication

Table 5 Selected dating evidence, period 5 (c AD 250 to ? early 5th century)

Land use	Context	Evidence	Description	Sherds	Date range
B7 (disuse)	[926]	pottery	AHFA 2F, 2V, 4M BUD internal; BB1 2 OL, 2F, 4M ARCX, 5J; BBS 2 AL, 2F; CC 3 ROD fine CGBL- or MOSL- like slip but fabric not fine enough; GROG 4M; MHAD; NVCC WBAD (?scroll) ROD, 1 'double' bead rim, possibly a flask, 4/5; OXRC 4DR38 profile, Young type C51; OXWC ?4P24 RPD; OXWW 7; PORD 2; ?SAMEG ?4DR38	49	350–400
B7 (disuse)	[1005]	pottery	AHFA 5J profile; BB2 2 AL, 4/5, 4H AL; BBS 2 OAL, 2A17; FINE 2F AL; OXRC; PORD 2; ?SAMEG 6DR33; VCWS 1B7–9	71	350–400
B21	[1376]	pottery	BB1 2 OL limescale; OXWW 7M22	3	250–400
B21 (disuse)	[1300]	pottery	PORD RLD	4	350–400
OA16	[85]	building material	2454, 2815, 3016		250–350
OA16	[300]	building material	2815, 3016		250–350
OA16	[352]	pottery	AHFA 2FX, 2V NCD, 4/5 BUD, 4M, 5J; BB1 5J; NVCC 5J; OXRC 4DR38; ?OXRC 5; OXWS 7; OXWW 7M22; PORD 2 RLD; SAMEG 4/5 BR	35	350–400
OA16	[248]	coin	<13>		(?340)–365
OA17	[1256]	pottery	AHFA 4M; OXRC 4 STD; OXWW 7M22	7	270–400

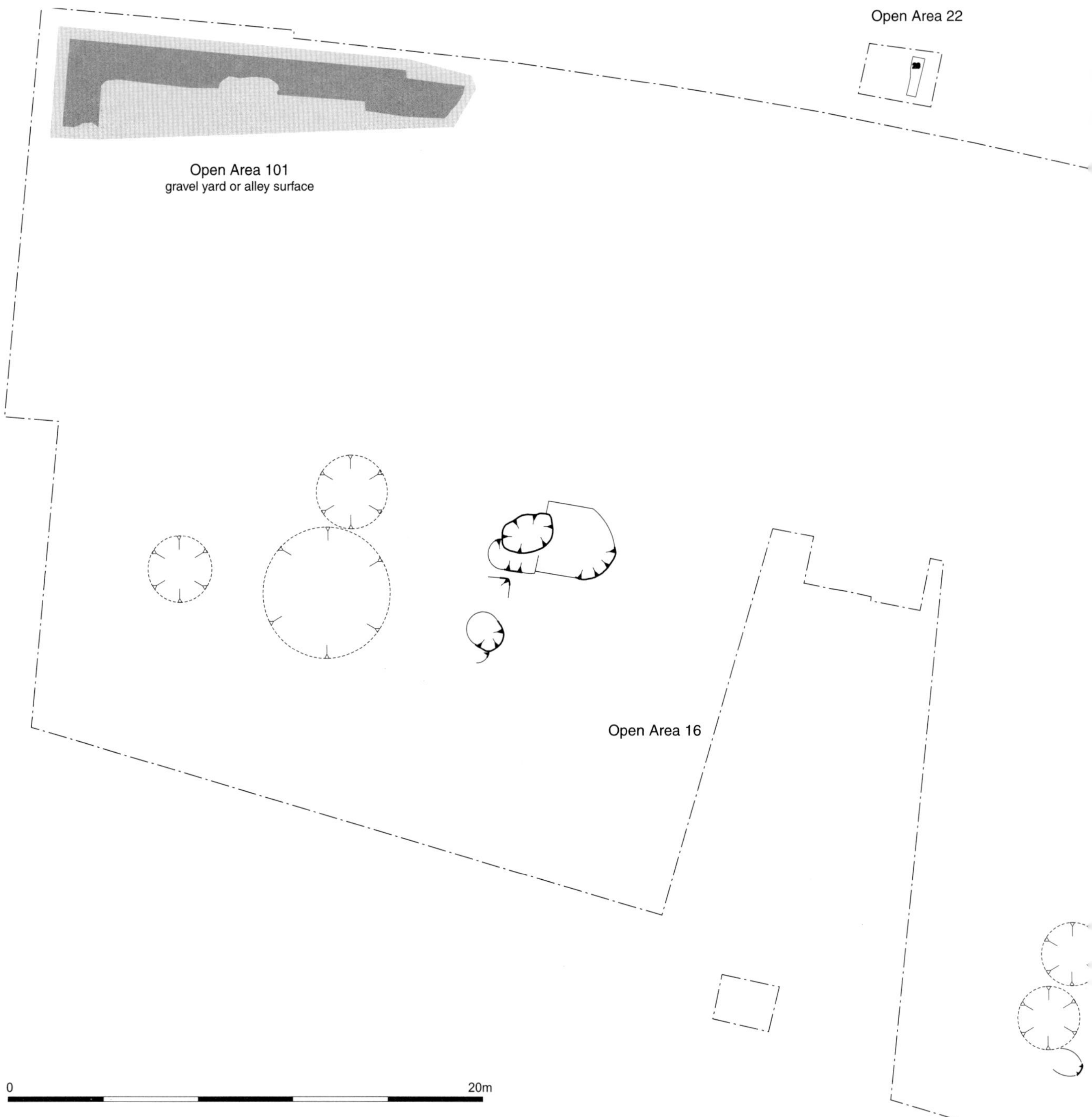

Fig 19 Plan of period 5 Roman or later pits and gravel surface in the western half of the site

that it belonged to a separate building. The floor subsequently slumped, forming a depression that was later crudely repaired with two thin layers of mortar patching.

Open Area 101: gravel yard or alley

An extensive rammed gravel surface, 100mm deep, was seen only in the 1954 watching brief, and considered too insubstantial to be a road. It contained one sherd of pottery dated to the 4th century AD. While this could be a 4th-century yard or alley surface, it is equally possible that it belongs to a later period.

Open Areas 16, 17 and 22: make-up cut by late Roman and/or later pits

Make-up was laid down and some 35 pits were dug. The majority of the pits appear to have been rubbish pits, with some cesspits. One pit contained four 3rd- or 4th-century coins and the remains of several dog skeletons. While most of the pits contained 3rd- or 4th-century dating material, it is quite possible that many of these features actually date from later periods but contained only residual Roman dating evidence. A small amount of Late Saxon pottery, originally interpreted

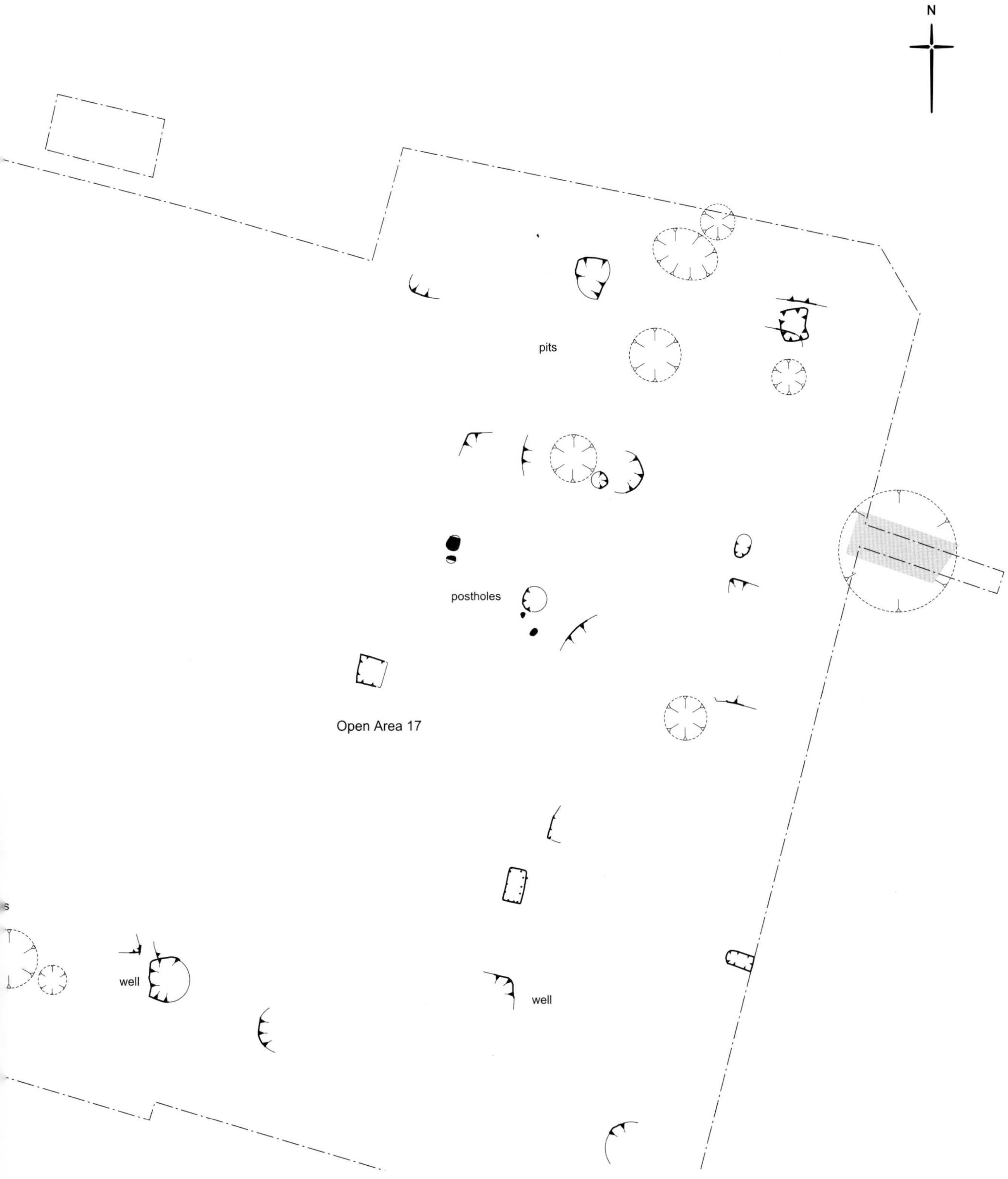

as intrusive, could indicate that some of these pits do in fact belong to period 7 (see 2.8 below). This includes imported Domburg-type ware, and very highly fired greyware, which could be an import from the Low Countries.

The pits in Open Area 16 produced the most substantial animal bone assemblage from those selected for detailed analysis: 1143 fragments. The bone derived mainly from equal components of ox or 'ox-sized' and sheep or goat, or 'sheep-sized' fragments, including definitely identified sheep, but with substantial components of pig and, particularly, dog. There were a few fragments of cat. There was limited recovery of domestic poultry: chicken, goose, and mallard or domestic duck. Foetal or

Fig 20 Detail of the partially robbed wall of Building 20, shown after the excavation of the robber cuts, but with the remains of the wall left in situ, from the south-east (0.5m scale)

neonate and infant pig bones were recovered from rubbish pit fills, one of which also produced an infant dog skeleton.

Wild 'scavenger' species were represented only by eight fragments of raven, probably derived from the same skeleton in one rubbish pit. Wild 'game' species were sparsely represented by a single fragment of red deer antler, and two fragments of roe deer radius and metatarsal. The pits also produced the most diverse and abundant sample of fish of those analysed in detail. These included freshwater (roach), migratory euryhaline species able to tolerate a wide range of salinities (eel and, possibly, flounder), and marine or estuarine species (herring family, cod family and plaice or flounder), but the bulk was derived from the cod family and plaice or flounder.

The only fragment of red deer was a piece of antler beam <209>, sawn through immediately proximal to a beam/tine junction, probably an offcut discarded after preparation of straight sections of antler beam for subsequent manufacture into artefacts such as combs (Pipe in prep). Although indicative of antlerworking at or close to the site, this find may well have derived from a shed antler and does not necessarily indicate consumption of red deer venison at the site. The same pit fill produced two fragments of roe deer; although neither of these bones showed butchery marks, their presence suggests consumption of roe deer venison from at least two individual animals.

The pits in Open Area 17 produced a much smaller assemblage of animal bone, similar to the preceding periods, but with a very sparse retrieval of poultry: two fragments of chicken and one of mallard or domestic duck. An ox horncore had been chopped through transversely at the base, indicating removal of the horn for subsequent removal and processing of the horn sheath as an industrial raw material.

Spelt wheat (*Triticum spelta* L) grains were present in a pit in Open Area 16, but did not occur in later deposits. Grains of bread/club wheat (*Triticum aestivum* L) were also present. These wheats are typical of those found in Roman London, spelt, in particular, having been recovered in large numbers from sites in the City (Davis in prep a; Davis in prep b). The lack of chaff and larger weed seeds, such as corncockle (*Agrostemma githago* L), suggests that this is waste from cleaning stored grain or a domestic store still with a small number of acceptable contaminants, which here included seeds of fat hen (*Chenopodium album* L) and campion/catchfly (*Silene* sp).

Edible fruit seeds included a mineralised plum/bullace (*Prunus domestica* L) stone and uncharred seeds of elderberry (*Sambucus nigra* L), fig (*Ficus carica* L) and blackberry (*Rubus fruticosus sensu lato*). These could have come from plants growing wild or in gardens. Elder produces large amounts of seed naturally, but elderberries do feature in Roman cookery, for example in a *patina* (pan) of elderberries, flavoured with pepper, liquamen (fish sauce), wine, *passum* (sweet raisin wine) and thickened with eggs (Apicius, 4.3.8, in Flower and Rosenbaum 1958, 103). Fig (*Ficus carica* L), however, would have been imported as dried fruit from the Mediterranean (Willcox 1977, 278).

Period discussion

The buildings

Building 7, and perhaps Buildings 6, 13, 14 and 15, were retained from the preceding period. The singular orientation of Building 20 was not matched by other buildings on the site, and currently defies explanation. With no evidence for the walls of Building 21, it is not possible to determine whether the orientation was shared by that structure.

While the extent of Building 21 is unknown, its construction clearly necessitated the demolition of Building 10, and extension of the new building across Open Area 100 between Buildings 10 and 17. If Building 17 had extended to the south of its room A, then it too must have been demolished in order to construct Building 21. If the new building occupied the whole area of its predecessors, it is possible that this structure extended across the whole of the eastern end of the site, a distance of more than 40m. The absence of any surviving walls from this structure is surprising, but can possibly be explained by the sporadic coverage of the areas of excavation in the eastern part of the site, and the extensive truncation from Saxon and later construction. In this context it is worth noting how little survived of Building 20.

The extent of the tessellated floors, and their better quality compared with their predecessors in Buildings 10 and 14, suggest a building of greater status than earlier structures. The buttresses added to Building 10 in period 4 suggest problems with subsidence, and the slumping of the floor of Building 21 room B shows that this continued to plague buildings at this location. The crude patching indicates that the building continued in use despite the slumping of the floor.

The animal bone assemblage from the pit fills

Alan Pipe

The particularly large and diverse animal bone assemblage from this period, especially that from Open Area 16, and to a lesser extent Open Area 17, mainly represents post-consumption waste, with a diet derived largely from beef with smaller, roughly equal components of mutton and pork, and very small contributions from chicken, goose, and mallard or domestic duck. There is definite evidence for the exploitation of a range of fish species, including those from fresh water and also the outer estuary and open sea. This implies the exploitation of a range of habitats, and the use of several different techniques for the capture of surface and mid-water dwelling (herring family) and demersal (dwelling on or near the seabed: plaice or flounder and cod family) species.

The consumption of a range of age classes within the major domesticates (ox, sheep or goat, and pig) provides direct evidence of the availability and use of a range of qualities of meat. This includes purpose-reared animals, as well as those slaughtered after use for a primary function such as dairying, wool production, traction or breeding. Indeed, the recovery of foetal remains also suggests that pigs were probably kept at, or close to, the site. Also, there is evidence for disposal of carcasses from species that had not been consumed, particularly dog and cat.

The recovery of raven, a scavenger species now extinct as a breeding wild bird in south-east England (Lack 1993, 376–7; Sharrock 1987, 290–1), suggests that carrion and refuse were available on ground surfaces, and that not all refuse was immediately disposed of in pits. The recovery of an offcut of sawn red deer antler and a chopped ox horncore, strongly suggests some level of antler- and hornworking in the vicinity. Red deer and roe deer were both widespread throughout Roman Britain (Yalden 1999, 128), primarily in woodland (Arnold 1994, 128–9, 134–5). They both provide good-quality venison.

Overall, these pits contained a mixture mainly of post-consumption refuse, together with small components of craft and industrial waste, and miscellaneous household detritus. It should be stressed that the striking differences in species presence and faunal diversity between this and the earlier periods may well be the result of uncertainties about the dating of the majority of the pits in Open Areas 16 and 17 (see above). Conversely, the assemblage is similar to that from period 7, reinforcing the suggestion that many of these pits are in fact of Saxon or Norman date, but contained only residual Roman dating evidence. The difference from the preceding periods may also be due, at least in part, to the much greater fragment count from period 5, rather than entirely a reflection of different patterns of animal exploitation. This period is also the earliest for which wet-sieved bulk samples were analysed in detail, and this may be responsible for the recovery of the fish species.

Stone mould for decorated pewter plates

Jackie Keily

Part of a stone mould <141>, probably for the production of pewter plates (Justine Bayley, pers comm), was found in the backfill of a Saxo-Norman building (B24, see 2.8 below), but was probably made after AD 250 (Fig 21; Fig 22). Although incomplete, the original mould was *c* 330mm in diameter and 53–64mm thick. The stone is a very fine limestone (Ian Betts, pers comm). The fragment comes from the upper portion of a circular mould, with a smooth, flat outer surface and a tooled straight outer edge. It has been very finely carved to form a mould for the decorated surface of a wide, flat rim. The decoration takes the form of a row of running animals, possibly dogs, with an inner plain indented line. There is an indented line of beading and a plain indented line running around the outer edge. The mould may not have been used as there are no signs of any residues, and may even have been unfinished.

Romano-British pewter largely dates to the late Roman period, with most objects coming from contexts dated to between *c* AD 250 and 410 (Beagrie 1989, 175). Metal vessels with relief beaded rims and repoussé decoration are known, for example the 4th-century Mildenhall treasure from Suffolk. In addition, similar running dogs and hunting scenes are found on cut decoration on 4th-century glass vessels (Price and Cottam 1998, 36–7, 125, fig 51a(ii)). For example, multi-layered moulds for the mass production of plain pewter plates were found at Silchester, where they are thought to represent one of the later industries in the town (Boon 1974, 273, fig 40 no. 4 and 274). Plain mould fragments have been found elsewhere in Britain (Beagrie 1989, 183–8, fig 4).

Stone moulds for pewter or lead/tin-alloy vessels are extremely rare in London. Excavations at Dominant House (DMT88) on the north bank of the Thames produced part of the base for a stack of stone moulds for making small lead/tin-alloy or pewter dishes. Little production waste has been found. Tin-alloy ingots were recovered from the Thames between Battersea and Wandsworth in the 19th century, and waste fragments have been found in Walbrook deposits to the east of the present site (Beagrie 1989, 188–9).

The present example is also unusual in having a decorated rim. The majority of the vessel moulds discussed by Beagrie (1989, 183–8) have no decoration surviving. On the few that do, such as those from Lansdown, Avon, the decoration is in the form of fluting, bead-and-reel or arcading, and is not figurative.

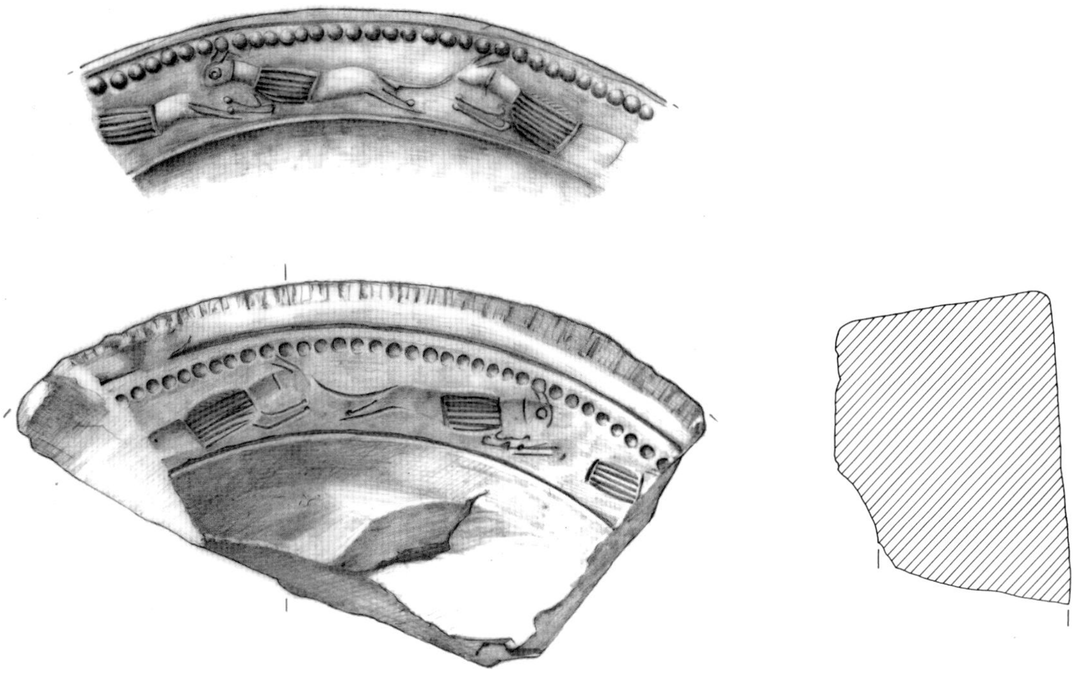

Fig 21 Part of the upper half of a stone mould <141>, probably for the production of pewter plates, with a rim decorated with running animals, possibly dogs. Probably of 4th-century date, but residual, found in the backfill of Building 24, period 7 (1:2)

Fig 22 Stone mould <141>, probably for the production of pewter plates (original diameter c 330mm)

2.7 Period 6: 'dark earth'

Open Area 18: 'dark earth'

Because of the depth of truncation caused by the 1954 building, 'dark earth' was only observed at one point, area watching brief 6 beneath modern Bread Street (not illustrated). Here the floor of Building 21 room B (see 2.6 above and Fig 18) was overlain by dark grey clayey silt, at least 0.20m thick, containing occasional fragments of mortar, apparently derived from the underlying Roman deposits.

However such material was deposited (see Watson 1998, 101–6, for a reappraisal of the various theories, and a reaffirmation of the conclusion that this represents abandonment), it clearly signals the end of the use of this building and also, apparently, of occupation on the site, as there is no evidence for any activity here between the 5th and 9th centuries. While it might be unwise to interpret a lack of activity merely from a lack of evidence, particularly on a site as heavily and extensively truncated as this, this lacuna corresponds with the historically attested abandonment of the Roman city during the Early Saxon period. The date of such an abandonment of the site cannot be determined, except that it must have been at some time after AD 365, but it is generally considered to have taken place in the early 5th century (eg Watson 1998, 100–1).

2.8 Period 7: Late Saxon and Saxo-Norman cellars and pits, AD 900–1140

The site was reoccupied in the 10th or 11th century, and by the mid 11th century four buildings with timber-lined cellars had been constructed (Fig 23). Several wells and a large number of rubbish and cesspits were also dug.

Building 22: timber-lined cellar

The evidence for Building 22 consisted of one corner of a heavily truncated timber-lined cellar, more than 0.76m deep, with a heavily decayed timber, probably plank, lining. The lining was supported by posts, which may have lain on wooden pads. At some point, presumably after the building had fallen into disuse, the lining had slumped inwards, along with the material backfilling the construction cut behind it. The nature of the original floor is uncertain: either a brickearth floor was replaced with a timber one, represented by a single surviving joist, or the brickearth was actually make-up for the timber floor.

There is no dating for the construction of this building, although it must postdate AD 300. A layer which might have been either occupation debris or the first dump of backfill in the cellar contained pottery dated to 970–1100, but which could be residual. Thus the disuse of this building might have occurred in the 11th century.

Building 23: timber-lined cellar

Although again heavily truncated, enough elements of the cellar forming Building 23 survived to calculate its original dimensions: *c* 14.4m x 5.3m, and originally more than 1.6m deep (Fig 24). One section of timber wall survived as stains up to 0.20m wide representing vertical planking (Fig 25), presumably stave-built cladding on the inside of a framework of posts set on the sill beams. The latter were heavily decayed, and *c* 0.25m wide by 80mm deep, and sat, at least partially, on pads of reused Roman tile and Kentish rag (Fig 26). Like Building 22, the material sides had slumped inwards. On the eastern side, at least, there was a second sill beam, or perhaps a joist, immediately inside the cladding.

A heavily decayed wooden floor had been laid on top of either a thin levelling or earlier floor of brickearth. This was pierced by a large number of stakeholes, and several postholes and shallow cut features. It is not possible to reconstruct a coherent layout of structures within the cellar, but it is likely that there was an alignment of posts along the long axis of the building (see Fig 24).

Uniquely for a Saxo-Norman building in London, two near complete pots had been buried beneath the floor (Fig 27; Fig 28; and see Fig 48); small parts of the rims had been broken off, apparently *in situ*. Pot <P4> in Early Medieval Sandy ware (EMS) was found empty, with its mouth covered with a fragment of Roman tile. Immediately above pot <P5> in Early Surrey ware (ESUR) lay two items: a fragment of folded lead sheet, *c* 32mm x 15mm <23>, and a fragment of iron, with an end that curves back on itself, possibly part of a candle holder <42>. The pot may have been covered by a piece of Kentish rag in a similar fashion to pot <P4>. Both pots had been used before being placed beneath the floor, with sooting present on the outside of pot <P4>. The top of pot <P5> lay some 50mm below the surviving level of the floor, and both pots appeared to have been sealed by the decayed wood and the brickearth.

Building 23 was apparently refloored: make-up was dumped, raising the level by *c* 0.25m, and was sealed by the second wooden floor, which also survived in a heavily decayed state. Alternatively, it is possible that these deposits actually represent parts of the wooden superstructure collapsing into the cellar during the decay or demolition of this building.

The fabrics of the two pots (EMS and ESUR) suggest a construction date for Building 23 between 1050 and 1100 (see Table 6). It is unclear at what date the building went out of use, although it was probably before 1150.

Building 24: timber-lined cellar

The south-western corner of another cellar, surviving to a depth of 0.69m, formed Building 24. Unlike Buildings 22 and 23, the sides had not slumped inwards, and consequently the construction technique was more apparent: the lining of heavily decayed vertical timbers, at least 10mm thick, lay on sill beams 0.18–0.26m wide and 80mm deep, in a construction cut which was packed with fragments of Kentish rag and soil. Although its southern end coincided with a wall of a late Roman building (B20, see 2.6 above), it did not share its orientation. It probably had a timber floor. There is no indication of the date at which this building was constructed, but its backfill contained pottery dating to 1050–1100, as did a pit which cut it. Thus the building probably went out of use in the late 11th, or possibly early 12th, century.

Building 25: ? timber-lined cellar

Heavily truncated structural remains may have formed a fourth timber-lined cellar, which survived to a depth of only *c* 0.5m. Two intercutting postholes lay against one edge of the cut, with what may have been a setting for more posts in the interior. While these features contained sherds of Late Saxon

Fig 23 Plan of period 7 timber-lined cellars and contemporary wells and pits

Shelly ware dated to 900–1050, suggesting a date for the disuse of this structure, it is possible that this was residual, and that it was somewhat later in date.

Open Areas 19, 20, 21, 102 and 103: pits and wells

Rubbish pits, with some cesspits and at least two wells, were dug in the areas around the buildings in period 7. Some of the pits described under period 5 may actually belong to this period (see 2.6 above). A ditch in Open Area 19 may have been a boundary associated with Building 24 which lay c 4m to the east. A pit in the same area produced 66 sherds from a single cooking pot in Early Medieval Sandy ware, with heavy external soot and thick white residue inside (Fig 29). The pits and well in Open Area 20 yielded sherds from up to 81 vessels, the majority in Late Saxon Shelly ware, Early Surrey ware and Early Medieval Sand-and-shell-tempered ware; mainly cooking pots and jars, but including a few bowls, pitchers and one sherd from a crucible. A pit in

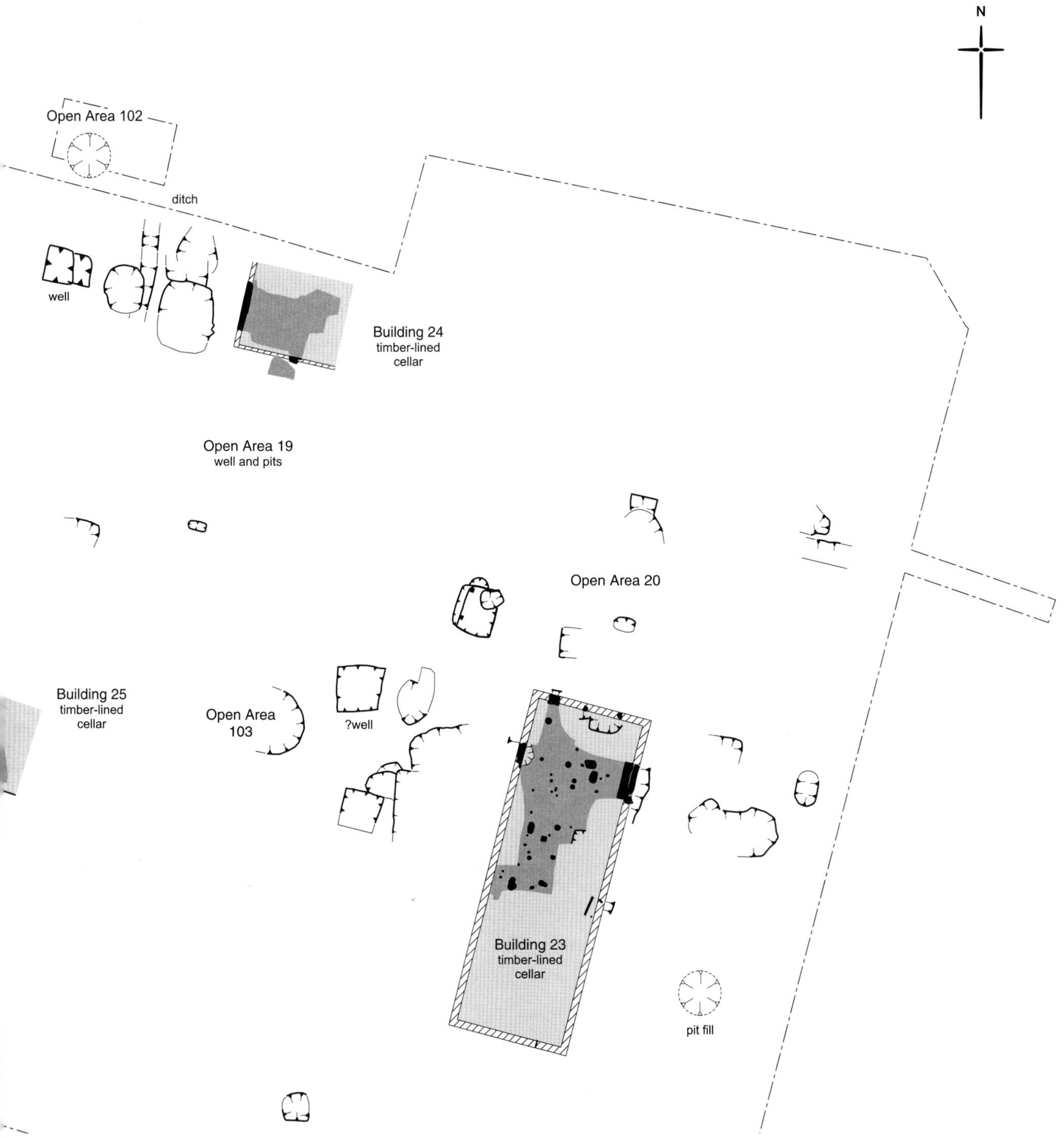

Open Area 20 produced a small fragment of a Late Saxon glass vessel <164> in natural blue glass, which probably dates to the 10th to 12th centuries.

Period discussion

The date of reoccupation of the site

There was no evidence for Saxon activity on the site before the 10th century, the earliest pottery types dating to after AD 900 and 970 (Table 6). Disuse deposits from Building 25 contained pottery dated to 900–1050. Similarly, Building 22 contained pottery dated to 970–1100, and thus its disuse probably dates to the 11th century. Their construction, therefore, may have taken place in either the 10th or 11th century. Some of the rubbish pits in Open Area 20 contained pottery dated to 900–1050, and these too could be of 10th- or 11th-century date. They are, however, probably contemporary with Building 23. The construction of that building is more closely dated, to *c* 1050–1100, by the two pots buried beneath the floor.

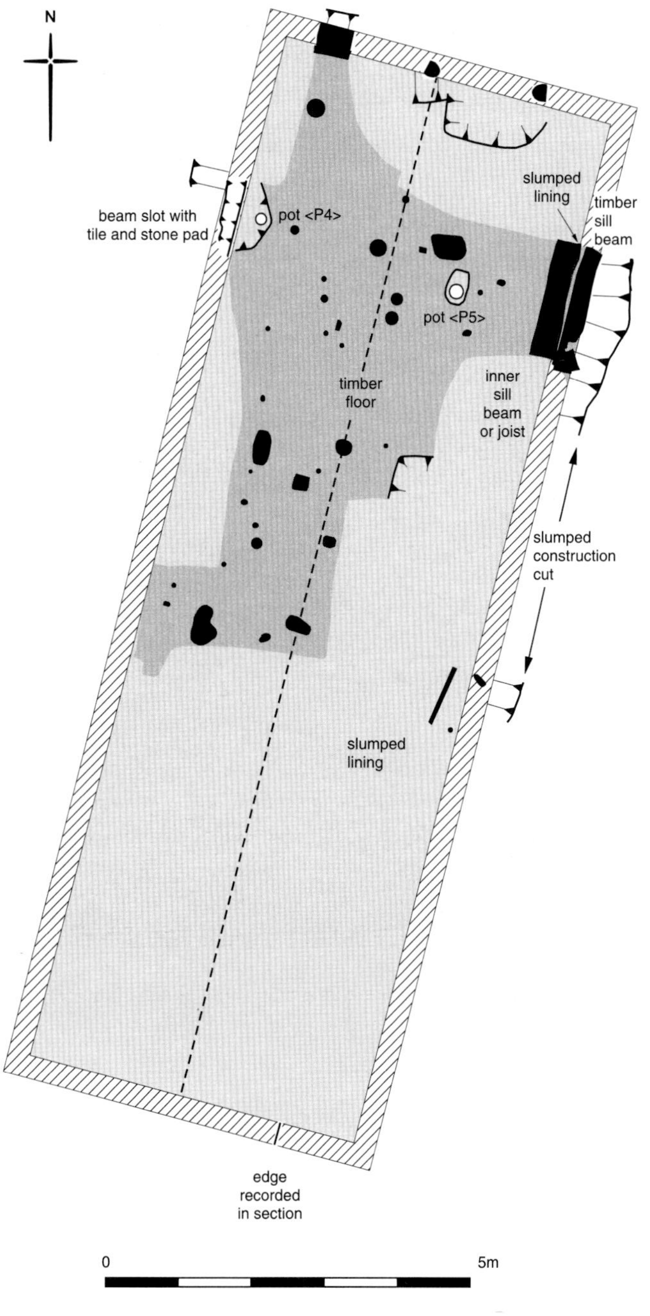

Fig 24 Plan of timber-lined cellar Building 23 showing pots deposited beneath the floor

Fig 25 Detail of vertical plank stains on the eastern side of timber-lined cellar Building 23, from the west (0.2m scale)

Fig 26 Detail of a pad for a sill beam, composed of reused Roman tile and stone fragments, in timber-lined cellar Building 23, from the north (0.2m scale)

Thus the buildings and associated features probably represent occupation which commenced in either the 10th or 11th century, and continued into the 11th and perhaps 12th centuries. Although this lacuna might be the result of the truncation of the Saxon ground surface and buildings without cellars, the lack of any pottery, even residual, that predates 900 does suggest a real lack of activity on the site up to at least that date, and probably 970 or 1000.

An early charter implies that Bread Street, immediately to the east of the site, was founded by the late 9th century (Schofield et al 1990, 154–5), although this might only apply to the southern end of the road, and other documentary references only date from c 1150–79 (Lobel 1989, 67). The uncertain dating of the Friday Street deposits is discussed below (see 2.9), but it is possible that it was established during period 7.

Fig 27 Pot <P4> deposited beneath the floor in timber-lined cellar Building 23, from the west. This pot was found empty, covered with a piece of reused Roman tile, and may well have originally been filled with a liquid offering

The range of pottery is on the whole typical of domestic occupation of the period (cooking pots, jars, bowls and pitchers). The greater part of a crucible was found in a pit in Open Area 20, and a complete Stamford ware crucible of the same date was also found in the 1954 fieldwork. These may indicate some light industry in the area. More intriguing is a complete Stamford ware sprinkler found in 1954 (Vince and Jenner 1991, no. 291), which may have had some liturgical function.

The buildings

Given the extent of truncation and slumping, and the poor preservation of the timbers, the construction techniques remain unclear, and it is even possible that the two sill beams of Building 23 belong to more than one building. Its method of construction, however, recalls that of a building at Watling Court, with a cellar lining on the inside of posts, which have been packed around with earth (Horsman et al 1988, 56–7). Building 22 appears to be more conventional, with posts inside the lining, and in Building 24 the lining may have been set into the sill beam, although it is possible that there may have been posts which did not survive in the earth and stone packing behind the lining.

Because the ground surface associated with the buildings was truncated, it is not possible to determine whether these were buildings with sunken floors, or with separate cellars. The use here of the term 'cellar' for these structures should

Table 6 Selected dating evidence, period 7 (AD 900–1140)

Land use	Context	Evidence	Description	Sherds	Date range
B23	[1210]	pottery	EMS complete pot buried beneath floor	2	1000–1100
B23	[1372]	pottery	ESUR complete pot buried beneath floor	1	1040–1150
B25	[131]	pottery	LSS	2	900–1050
OA19	[638]	pottery	LSS	46	900–1050
OA19	[652]	pottery	EMCH; EMIS; EMS; EMSH; EMSS; ESUR; LCOAR; REDP OLV	31	1080–1100
OA19	[658]	pottery	EMS	71	970–1100

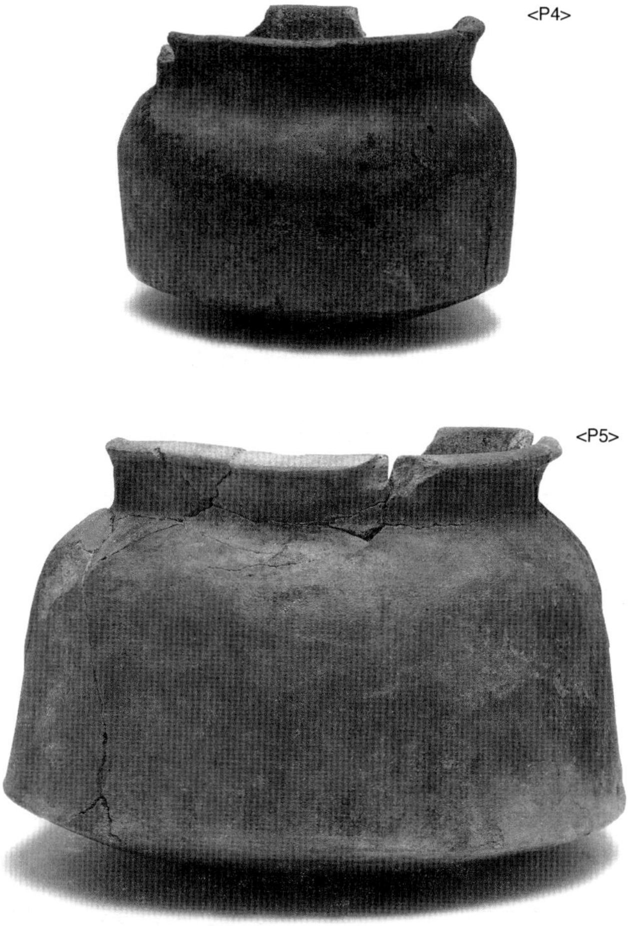

Fig 28 Pots <P4> fabric EMS (diameter 138mm) and <P5> fabric ESUR (diameter 194mm), deposited beneath the floor in timber-lined cellar Building 23

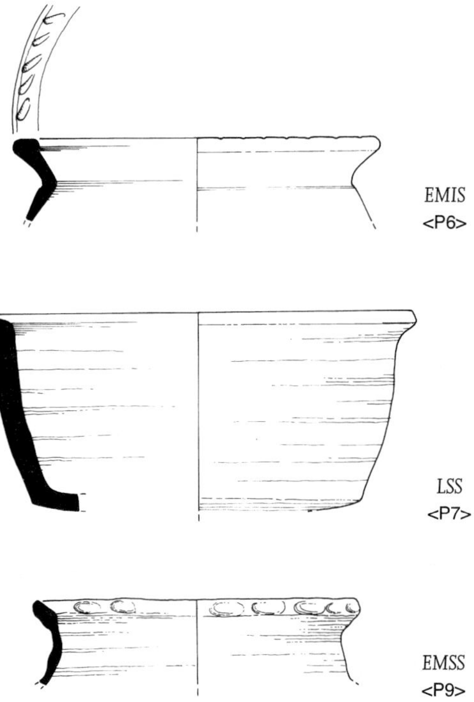

Fig 29 Saxo-Norman pottery – these examples were residual in the fills of later pits in Open Areas 19 and 20, period 8 (1:4)

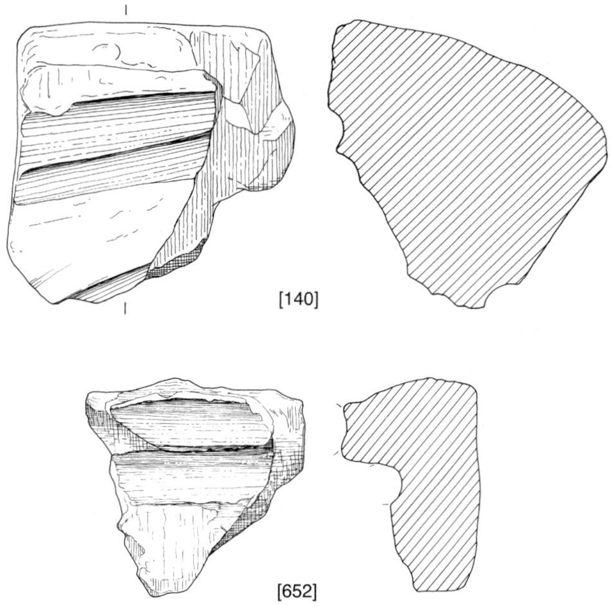

Fig 30 Daub fragments recovered from Building 25 and a pit in Open Area 19 (1:2)

not be taken to imply an interpretation one way or another. The depth of Building 23, however, more than 1.6m, does suggest a separate cellar for that building, at least.

A small quantity of burnt daub was recovered from Building 25 and Open Area 19 (Fig 30). It can be distinguished from Roman daub by its larger size and lack of abrasion. The daub from Building 25 has a flat base and a curved edge, with the remains of round wattle impressions. It may have come from a doorway or other opening. Two fragments with a flat surface and wattle marks, probably from the walls of a building, were found in a rubbish pit in Open Area 19, adjacent to Building 24. This is the only evidence for the superstructures of these buildings. Although the small quantities recovered could have been introduced from outside the site, they suggest that some buildings had timber frames with wattle and daub infill, rather than an all-timber construction.

The walls of Buildings 23 and 24 suggest a 'stave-built' construction, although this may simply have been the form of the lining of the cellars, and not have reflected the construction above ground level. It has been noted that stave-building first appears in London in the 11th century (Horsman et al 1988, 75), which is consistent with the dating of Building 23.

Buildings 22 and 23, and probably Building 24, had timber floors, but there was no evidence for the floor of Building 25. These floors may have been replacements for earlier brickearth floors, or the brickearth may have been bedding for the timber. The floor of Building 22 was laid on joists, while that of Building 23 had been raised and refloored, both possibly measures to counter damp. There was no evidence for entrances, nor for internal features such as hearths or ovens, but the plethora of stakeholes in Building 23 demonstrates the presence of some structures within that building, possibly partitions.

The pots buried beneath the cellar floor of Building 23

Lyn Blackmore

The burial of votive offerings beneath buildings is known from the Roman period (Merrifield 1965, 54, 277, no. 287), but no other complete vessels of Late Saxon or medieval date have been found in similar circumstances on published sites in the City (Merrifield 1969, 100; Horsman et al 1988; Vince and Jenner 1991; Schofield et al 1990; Hill and Woodger 1999).

If the pots were sealed beneath the floor, as appeared to be the case, then it is hard to see how they can have had any practical purpose. They could have served the same purpose as Roman votive deposits and the later witch bottles (Merrifield 1969, 100; Maloney 1980), which were intended to protect the owner and ward off evil. The void inside pot <P4> could have originally held a liquid offering, such as wine or beer, but it is not possible to identify the functions of the lead and iron objects associated with pot <P5>.

Complete pots have been found in later contexts in London, but all were associated with churches. The three complete empty late 13th-century jugs found at All Hallows Lombard Street were standing in the cavity of an empty wall (Merrifield 1969, 100). The jugs from All Hallows may have contained charms or prayers, as a possible piece of parchment was found in a similar context in a church in Bexley (Merrifield 1969, 100). Complete pots which may have been foundation deposits have been found on at least three 17th-century sites in London; two are associated with churches, while one is associated with the gatehouse at Aldgate (Merrifield 1969, 100–1). If the finds from 25 Cannon Street are to be interpreted as foundation vessels, then their proximity to St Paul's and the early church of St Werburga (later St John the Evangelist) may be significant.

Alternatively, if the pots were buried for some more practical purpose, they may have been used to store provisions which were to be kept cool, or for some medicinal or alchemical purpose. No records survive for such practices at this early date, but several later medieval recipes survive which require pots to be buried, and sometimes left over a period of time. In many cases two pots were involved, with an upper one draining into a lower one which was buried in a small pit. Four different combinations used for distillation and fermentation processes are illustrated by Moorhouse (1981, 117–18), one of which shows an upper pot with multi-perforated base which drains into a lower pot; the rim of the lower pot is at ground level, unlike those from Building 23, and flanked by tiles on which a fire is set, while the upper pot is covered by a tile (Moorhouse 1981, fig 90D). This would probably have been outside, rather than inside, a building (in some cases the pots had to be buried in, or sealed with, horse dung), but it must be assumed that the tradition had evolved over many generations, and different practices may apply for different periods or recipes. It is, therefore, possible that the two pots found in this building were part of a composite arrangement used for a similar purpose.

Ingot mould

Jackie Keily

A fragment of Roman brick was reused as an ingot mould <215> (Fig 31) in the Late Saxon/early medieval period, and was found with residual pottery dating to AD 900–1150, in a later feature (S1, see 2.9 below). The indentation for the ingot is 40mm long and 10mm wide, tapering slightly at each end, cut into the upper, smoothed surface of the brick. The sides of the indent slope inwards towards the base and the inner surface is burned and blackened. X-ray fluorescence analysis of the mould by David Dungworth of the Centre for Archaeology produced evidence for the presence of zinc and lead in and around the cavity, as well as trace elements of copper and tin. It is thought that it was probably used for casting copper alloys, and therefore is indicative of metalworking in the vicinity of the site. Similar moulds have been found elsewhere in London from Late Saxon contexts, at Guildhall Yard (Keily 1997) and Milk Street (Pritchard 1991, 166–7), largely dating to the 10th–11th centuries, as well as elsewhere in Britain (eg Coppergate, York and Flaxengate, Lincoln; Justine Bayley, pers comm).

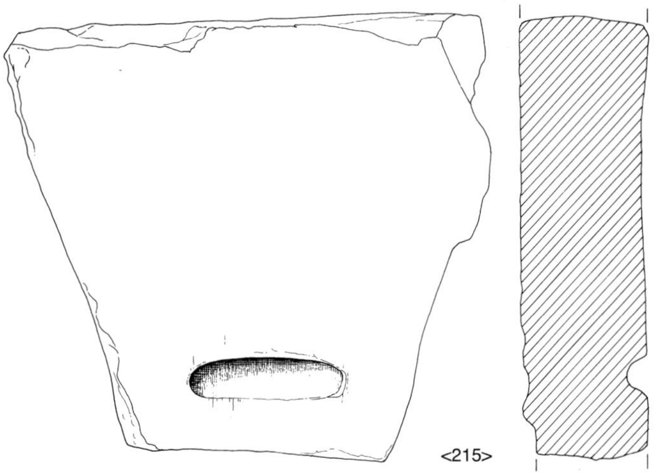

Fig 31 A fragment of a Roman brick <215> reused as a metalworking mould for small ingots. It is probably of 10th- or 11th-century date, but was found in Structure 1, period 8 (1:2)

Imported pottery

Lyn Blackmore

The site lies a short distance to the north of Queenhithe, the first landing place and market to be created in Late Saxon London. This is reflected in the presence of non-local and imported pottery typical of the 10th and 11th centuries in Open Areas 19 and 20. Sherds of Domburg-type ware, a very rare find in London, and the very highly fired greyware, which could be an import from the Low Countries, were present in the pits of Open Area 16, period 5, though they may well have derived from period 7 activity. Originally interpreted as intrusive material, the pits could date to this period (see 2.6 above). The range and increasing amount of such imported pottery in the City reflects the growth of contemporary trade in the 10th and 11th centuries, and the fact that from c 1000 merchants from France, Germany and the Low Countries were regularly visiting London (Vince 1985, 42; Blackmore 1999a; Blackmore 1999b).

Food remains

Lisa Gray and Alan Pipe

The small charred grain assemblage from a well in Open Area 20, a few metres from Building 23, differs from the Roman samples only in the absence of spelt wheat (*Triticum spelta* L) and presence of barley (*Hordeum sativum* L), while a pit beneath the floor of that building contained oats (*Avena* spp). The abundance of elderberry (*Sambucus nigra* L) seeds in these features could be due to differential preservation, because of the tough woody testa protecting the seed. Medieval and later herbals, however, list a number of uses for the berries, leaves, flowers and bark of the elder tree, so it is plausible that these elderberry seeds are the remains of making medicinal elderberry wine or cordial (Culpeper 1653, 127–30; Grieve 1994, 265–78; Mabey 1977, 74).

The substantial and diverse assemblage of animal bone is dominated by ox with smaller and roughly equal components of sheep or goat and pig. There is evidence of a range of age classes, again suggesting a range of available meat qualities, and for occasional consumption of domestic poultry: chicken and, to a lesser extent, goose. Consumption of wild 'game' species is indicated only by two fragments of woodcock from Open Areas 20 and 21.

Open Areas 19 and 20 both produced evidence for working of sheep or goat horn in the vicinity. A partial horse skeleton from the fill of a rubbish pit in Open Area 20 shows a transverse chop mark at the distal astragalus, the 'ankle' joint, which may have been inflicted during removal of the hide, the only butchery marks on any horse bone. Recovery of foetal/neonate pig bones and infant sheep or goat bones from Open Area 20 suggests the stalling of pigs and sheep or goats may have taken place at or close to the site.

The fish remains from this period exhibit a somewhat greater diversity of species than earlier material, including ray (probably roker/thornback ray), smelt, gurnard and mackerel in very small numbers, which were not present in period 5. Otherwise they closely resemble those from period 5 in overall composition, suggesting the same overall pattern of fish exploitation. The assemblage is dominated by cod family and plaice/flounder, including a butchered dentary (lower jaw) of a cod of c 0.85m length/5kg gutted weight. Both periods produced eel, clupeid (herring family), roach and cyprinid (carp family).

2.9 Period 8: early medieval construction, Friday Street and the church of St Werburga, 1140–1230

Friday Street and the church of St Werburga were in existence by the late 12th century, but both may have originated earlier. There is evidence for at least six other early medieval buildings, and for rubbish and cesspits in the open spaces around them (Fig 32; Fig 33).

Road 1: Friday Street surfaces

The gravel surfaces of an early medieval road, more than 0.50m deep, were seen only in one testpit. The approximate alignment in the figures has been constructed from these surfaces and from medieval and post-medieval building lines, including the church of St Werburga. The earliest road surface observed continued below the limits of excavation, and there may well have been earlier road surfaces beneath that. This layer, and thus the road, appears to date from after 1180 (Table 7), but if a single jug handle were intrusive, then this surface might have been constructed as early as 1050, that is, during period 7. A post-1180 date corresponds to the earliest documentary reference to Friday Street, between 1138 and 1160 (Lobel 1989, 74). The date at which the road actually originated remains unknown, awaiting future excavation of those deposits preserved *in situ*.

As one of the few untruncated ground surfaces seen in the excavations, it is worth noting that the earliest surface of the road lay at 13.10m OD, c 1.0m above the Roman tessellated floor of Building 21 room B, and some 3.3m below modern ground level.

Building 103: early phase of church of St Werburga

The church of St Werburga (also spelt Wereburga or Werburge) (Fig 32) was named after an 8th-century Mercian princess who became abbess of Ely (Harben 1918, 620). The church is understood to have been established by 1098–1108 (Schofield 1994, 106). The remains of the church were seen only in the 1954 fieldwork. The structure postdated deposits containing pottery dated to c 970–1150, and lay on a different orientation from the buildings of period 7.

The walls of the church were composed of Kentish rag, on a foundation of Kentish rag rubble, probably robbed from Roman structures, and gravel. An early floor of the nave was composed of a mixture of mortar and gravel. There may have been a buttress supporting the south wall of the nave, although it was far less substantial than the main foundations, and may belong to an earlier structure.

There is insufficient information to allow a date to be assigned to most of the features within the church. A skeleton within the nave was noted as an 'early burial', as was a chalk

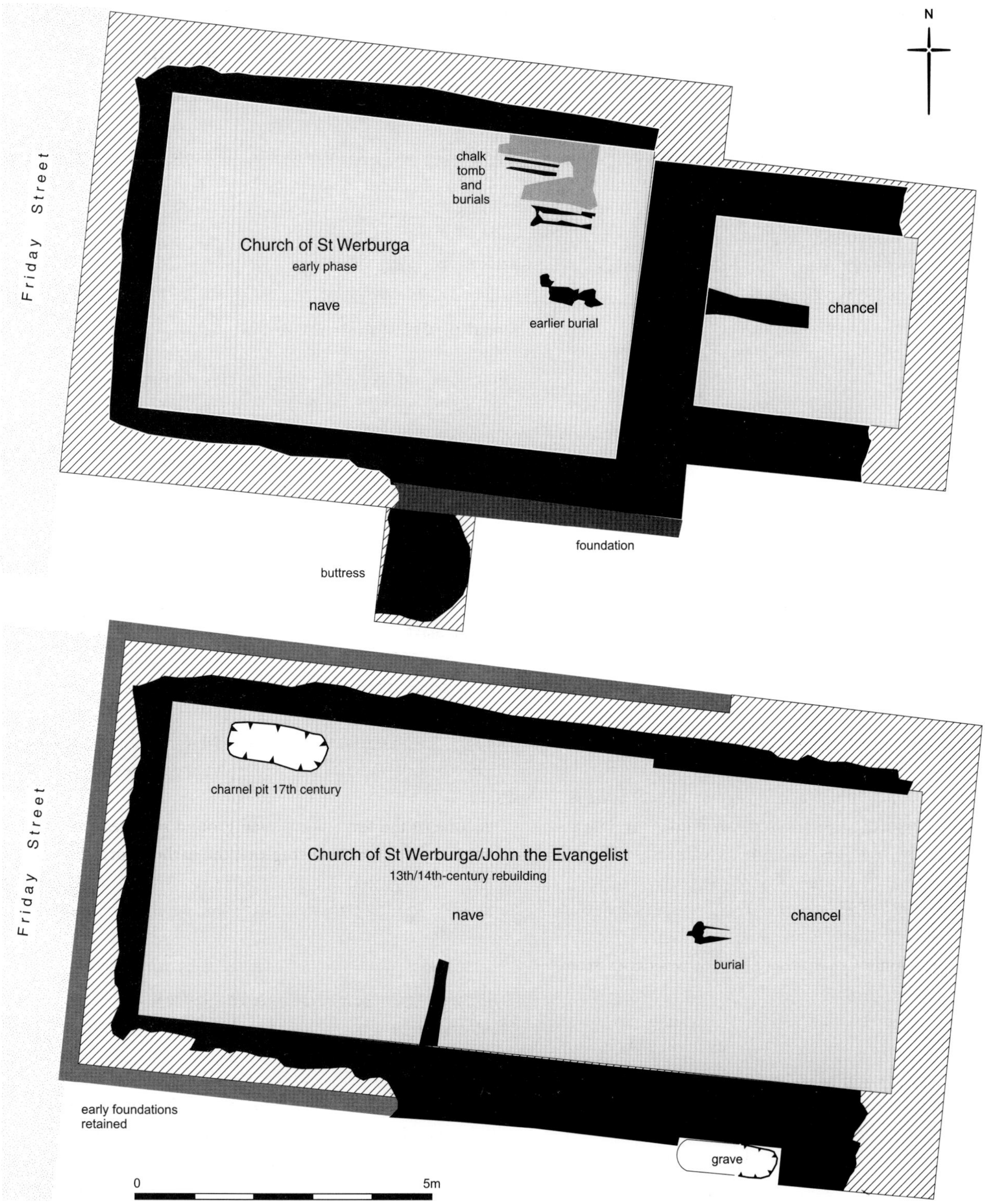

Fig 32 The church of St Werburga, later St John the Evangelist

Table 7 Selected dating evidence, period 8 (1140–1230)

Land use	Context	Evidence	Description	Sherds	Date range
R1	[40]	pottery	EMSH; EMSS; ESUR; LOND; NFRY	9	1180–1280
OA19	[694]	pottery	ESUR; LCOAR SHEL; LOND; LOND EAS; LSS; SHER; SSW	33	1150–1200
OA24	[77]	pottery	EMCH; EMS; EMSS; ESUR; KING; LCOAR; LCOAR CALC; LOGR; NFRY; SATH; STAM; THET	108	1140–50
OA24	[173]	pottery	LIMP; LOND; LOND NFR; SHER	8	1180–1270
OA25	[194]	pottery	EMGR; EMIS; EMS; EMSH; EMSS; ESUR; LCALC; LCOAR; LCOAR CALC; LOGR; LOND ROU; NEOT; REDP OLV; SHER; SSW; THET	114	1140–50

Fig 33 Plan of period 8 buildings and pits, including the church of St Werburga

tomb which contained one or two other skeletons. Another burial in what is recorded as an 'early coffin' lay immediately to the east of the wall between the nave and chancel.

Open Area 23: make-up

Make-up (not illustrated) was laid over earlier pits in the western part of the site, in advance of the construction of Buildings 26, 28 and 29, as well as the pits of Open Areas 24 and 26.

Buildings 26, 27 and 32: chalk and gravel foundations

The lowest part of Building 26 was composed of gravel, with heavily decayed planks laid on its surface, and then a further 40mm of gravel. Above this lay a 0.28m thick layer of roughly faced chalk blocks, sealed in turn by another layer of gravel, 50mm thick. On this foundation the main wall of roughly dressed stone blocks, with occasional lumps of chalk and flint, was laid in rough courses. Buildings 32 and 27 were similar

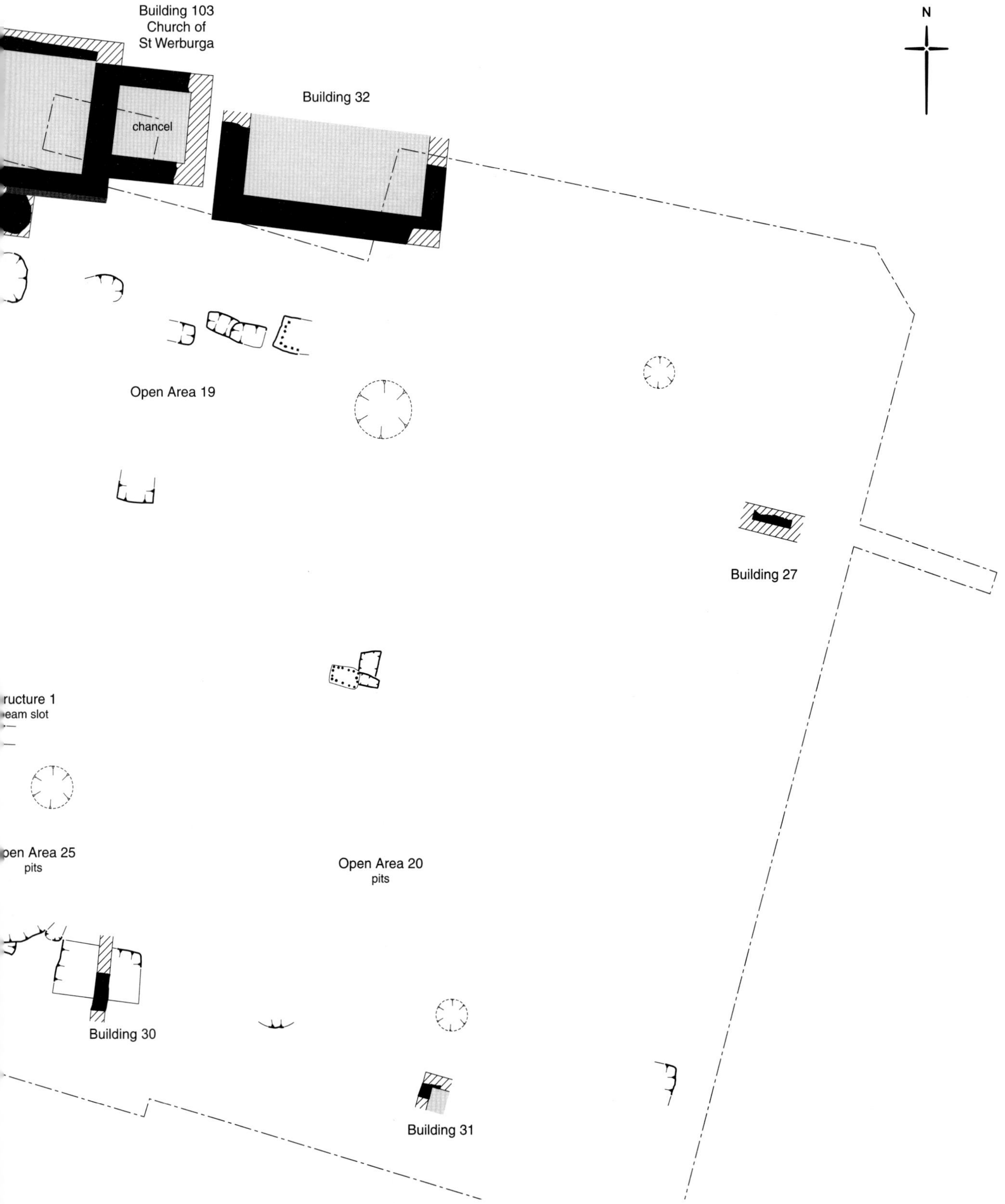

chalk foundations with gravel layers. This construction technique, with minor variations, has been recorded on nearby sites at Milk Street, dated to 1100–1230, and Watling Court, dated to 1100–1200. None of the three structures was dated, but this form of construction is thought to have been in vogue from the 11th to the early 13th centuries (Schofield et al 1990, 164–5, fig 54).

Buildings 28–31

The robbed beam slot forming Building 28 lay parallel to the reconstructed alignment of Friday Street, and may have formed the rear of a building fronting on to that road. Building 29 took the form of one corner of a chalk foundation or post pad, which lay mostly beyond the limits of excavation.

The rather more substantial foundation of Building 30 was composed of a mixture of Kentish rag, chalk and reused fragments of Roman tile, and lay parallel to the reconstructed alignment of Friday Street. Building 31 was the roughly built corner of a chalk cellar, or possibly a cesspit lining. Both could date from this period or later.

Open Areas 19, 20, 24, 25 and 104: pits; Open Area 26: levelling; ?Structure 1

Much of Open Areas 19 and 20 continued to be used for the disposal of rubbish and cess, some pits being lined with wattle or wood. This activity was also carried out in Open Areas 24, 25 and 104, presumably in open yards or gardens behind the houses along the street frontages. At least one well was dug in Open Area 24.

The pottery assemblage recovered from these Open Areas, c 500 sherds, is dominated by cooking pots, with some pitchers, suggesting that this is domestic refuse from nearby houses. Three fragments of stone querns were found <178> <197> <198>. Two were made from lava stone from the Mayen region of northern Germany, and may be Roman rather then medieval as this trade dates back to the Roman period. Botanical remains from the pits of Open Area 24 produced a similar assemblage to that from period 7, except that no barley was found. The pits of Open Areas 19 and 24 produced a small assemblage of animal bone suggesting the consumption mainly of beef, with smaller quantities of mutton and pork, goose, chicken and plaice/flounder. A goat horncore had been chopped through transversely at the base, indicating deliberate detachment from the skull. This was probably for subsequent removal of the horn sheath as a raw material, and suggests some level of hornworking in the locality.

Structure 1 was perhaps a beam slot or other structural element, possibly within Open Area 25, or a more substantial building. It may have dated from this period or later. Open Area 26 (not illustrated) was a further horizon of make-up, laid down over the pits of Open Area 24 and cut by another pit. This may represent the levelling over and sealing of the earlier pits, in preparation for yet another bout of refuse disposal.

Period discussion

The church of St Werburga (B103) and Building 32 shared an orientation at right angles to Friday Street, and lay parallel to medieval Aethelingestraete – corresponding to modern Watling Street – immediately to the north of the site. The latter is known to have been in existence by 1230 (Harben 1918, 615).

Building 28 lay c 12.5m to the west of the reconstructed line of Friday Street and parallel to it, and Building 30 the same distance to the east. This distance may correspond to regular building sizes on either side of that road. A similar regularity was noted in alignments of pits at Watling Court, which were situated c 12m back from the street frontages, and presumed to reflect the depth of the buildings (Schofield et al 1990, 45–6).

The pottery from period 8 differs from that in period 7 in that it includes larger groups of material and more imports. Notable pieces include a perforated handle fragment from a curfew in Shelly Sandy ware <P21> (Blackmore in prep), a London-type ware sherd with ring-and-dot stamps in an unusual quatrefoil arrangement with a fifth stamp at the centre <P18>, and an unusual decorated handle from a north French jug <P22> (Fig 34).

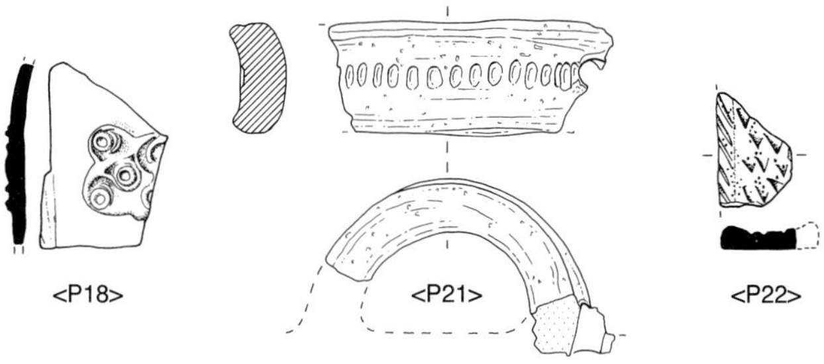

Fig 34 Pottery from the fills of pits in Open Area 25 and Road 1, period 8: London-type ware sherd with ring-and-dot stamps <P18>; perforated handle fragment from a curfew in Shelly Sandy ware <P21>; decorated handle from a north French jug <P22> (1:4)

2.10 Period 9: later medieval pits and buildings, 1230–1440

The church of St Werburga was rebuilt with a wider chancel, and there is evidence for the construction of more buildings, as well as several substantial masonry-lined cesspits (Fig 35).

Building 103: rebuilding of church of St Werburga/John the Evangelist

By 1356 the dedication of the church had been changed to the more prosaic St John the Evangelist (Harben 1918, 323). All three walls of the nave were rebuilt on their original alignments, and the chancel widened by rebuilding the north and south walls to form continuations of the nave (see Fig 32). The chancel increased in width from c 3.1m to 4.95m, slightly less than the 5.1m width of the nave. This difference may suggest that the rebuilding was carried out at two different times. At the south-eastern corner of the chancel, the wall projected southwards by 0.60m, possibly as part of a buttress. A grave was located neatly in the angle of the wall and this projection, and is therefore unlikely to have predated the rebuilding. The grave contained pottery dated to 1270–1350, and itself cut a deposit producing pottery dated to c 1140 to 1180 or 1200. The rebuilding, therefore, probably took place in the 13th or 14th century, although not necessarily at the same time as the rededication.

The floor of the church was paved with tiles at least once, perhaps twice. One plain yellow glazed 'Westminster' tile made c 1240–1300, and two decorated tiles made at Penn in Buckinghamshire between c 1350 and 1390 (Eames 1980, nos E2343, E2537), were found set into the same floor. This is by no means uncommon; a similar combination was excavated at the church of St Botolph, Billingsgate (Betts 1994, 136). Either a 13th-century floor was replaced in the late 14th century with Penn tiles, and some of the old 'Westminster' tiles were reused alongside the new ones, or worn parts of an earlier floor were repaired in the following century. There is no evidence to suggest that these refloorings took place at the same time as the rebuilding of the church, although all of these works fall within *c* 1200–1400.

Decorated tiles of both 'Westminster' and Penn types were recovered from the graveyard of the church and the surrounding area, and very probably came from the church. The 'Westminster' tiles probably date to the 1240s, or in one case the 1250s or later. The latter is of particular importance as it shows a design not so far found on any other 'Westminster' floor tile (Betts in prep). It shows a yellow beast, almost certainly a lion, standing over a serpentine, dotted, yellow motif which probably represents a snake, within a yellow quadrant band *c* 17mm wide which is decorated with regularly spaced brown dots (Fig 36). This tile would have formed part of a four-tile panel, with a design of beasts within a roundel 0.28m in diameter. Other tiles of both types have been published previously (Eames 1980, nos 2037, ?2552, 2334; Hohler 1942, nos 74, ?75).

Later features within the church included the lower half of a skeleton, lying partially over the foundation separating the nave and chancel, and an interior wall which had been partly removed by an 18th-century vault. In addition to the grave to the south of the nave, mentioned above, disturbed human bones lying to the south of the chancel may also have dated from this period.

Building 33: foundation; Building 34: cellar west of Friday Street

Building 33 consisted of Kentish rag, chalk, flint and reused Roman and medieval roofing tile foundation, a vestige of a return surviving at the northern end. It replaced Building 28 from period 8, but was apparently on a very slightly different alignment, not reflected in adjacent features. Building 34 was the chalk and Kentish rag wall of a cellar on the western side of Friday Street, opposite the church of St Werburga.

Open Areas 19, 20, 27 and 28: pits

The pits of Open Area 26 were sealed with a further levelling of the pit fills, or make-up, in advance of the excavation of more rubbish and cesspits, two of which were probably lined with wattle supported by large stakes. A pit in Open Area 27 contained a copper-alloy fragmentary pendant, with traces of gilding <51> (Fig 37). A later phase of activity, Open Area 28, included a well and a very large rubbish pit, or pits, excavated against the foundation of Building 26, which continued in use into the 17th century. Open Area 19 included the western side of a ragstone-lined cesspit.

The objects discarded in the Open Area 28 pits (Fig 38; Fig 39) include a number of Dutch Redware cauldrons and pipkins which suggest the presence of a 15th-century kitchen nearby, Rhenish Stoneware drinking vessels and other tablewares, and a urinal. A pottery money box dating from the 15th century was recovered whole; a single sherd, which had been broken out to remove the money, was replaced inside it before it was thrown away (see Fig 39).

Structures 3, 4 and 100: masonry cesspits

Structure 3 was a substantial cesspit, lined with chalk and Kentish rag, a few blocks of the latter having been burned before reuse in this structure. The earlier linings on the west and east sides, 0.20m thick, had slumped towards the centre at some point (Fig 40), and new linings had been rebuilt behind them in a more substantial form, 0.50m thick. Arches surviving within the masonry on the southern and western sides suggest a vaulted roof.

Pottery from the cesspit included 50 sherds from a single baluster jug which must have smashed when it landed in the pit. The pottery dates ranged from the late 13th to 15th centuries, implying that the pit was in use for a considerable length of time. The pit was probably constructed after 1270, and used until at least 1480, and possibly into the 16th century.

The cesspit contained the wooden handle of an iron scale-tang knife <5>, with decorative copper-alloy rivets and fittings, which dates to the 15th or 16th century (see Fig 37), and a copper-alloy mount <19> with a five-petalled flower motif, probably a rose, dating to the 14th or 15th century. It also contained a group of imported vessels, mainly drinking vessels, of 14th- to 16th-century date, including fine vessels from southern France and northern Europe (see Fig 37). The relatively large quantity of glass includes fragments of two glass hanging lamps, dating from the 13th century to the Dissolution <124–6> and <137>; an imported prunted beaker, with an out-turned rim and applied thread trail decoration, dating to the 15th–16th centuries <135>; a *Krautstrunk* or cabbage stalk beaker with large applied prunts on the body and applied pinched trails, dating to the late 15th or 16th century and probably northern European in origin, possibly Rhenish <127>; and part of the bowl of a colourless stemmed drinking vessel with applied and marvered trails of thin opaque white glass dating to the 14th or 15th century and probably from southern France <134>. Imported French glass of this period is extremely rare. The later fills contained a near complete stemmed drinking vessel, dating to the late 15th or 16th century <138>. This is a very high-quality vessel and may be an imported Italian piece. The metal of the glass, however, is not of the finest quality and it may, therefore, be *façon de Venise*, made by one of the many Venetian glassworkers who came to London from the late 16th century.

Structure 4 was a cesspit solidly constructed of Kentish rag, and trapezoidal in plan. The orientation of the northern side lay at right angles to Bread Street, but that of the remaining sides probably reflected an unknown building

Fig 35 Plan of period 9 structures, including the church of St Werburga/St John the Evangelist

or land division, and was reflected in the later Buildings 37 and 38 (see 2.11 below). Like Structure 3, the pit may have been in use from the late 13th or early 14th century through to a date after 1480, and perhaps as late as the Great Fire of 1666. It produced part of a Siegburg Stoneware drinking jug of the type known as a jakobakanne, and part of the base of a glass urinal <118>. The latter are a frequent find on medieval sites and were used in urinoscopy, the study of the colour and clarity of a patient's urine for medical diagnosis (Keys 1998, 252–4). The pit also contained part of the neck and base of a diagonally ribbed (writhen) bottle dating to the 13th–16th centuries <166>.

Structure 100 was a group of heavily truncated ragstone walls which may have formed parts of a cesspit similar to others constructed during this period.

Period discussion

There is little evidence for new buildings during this period, but the advent of several substantial masonry-lined cesspits suggests that this is the result of truncation. Building 30, and perhaps Buildings 27, 29 and 31, may have continued in use. Cesspit Structure 100, the cesspit in Open Area 19 and the northern side of cesspit Structure 4 shared an orientation that differs slightly from that of the church of St Werburga and

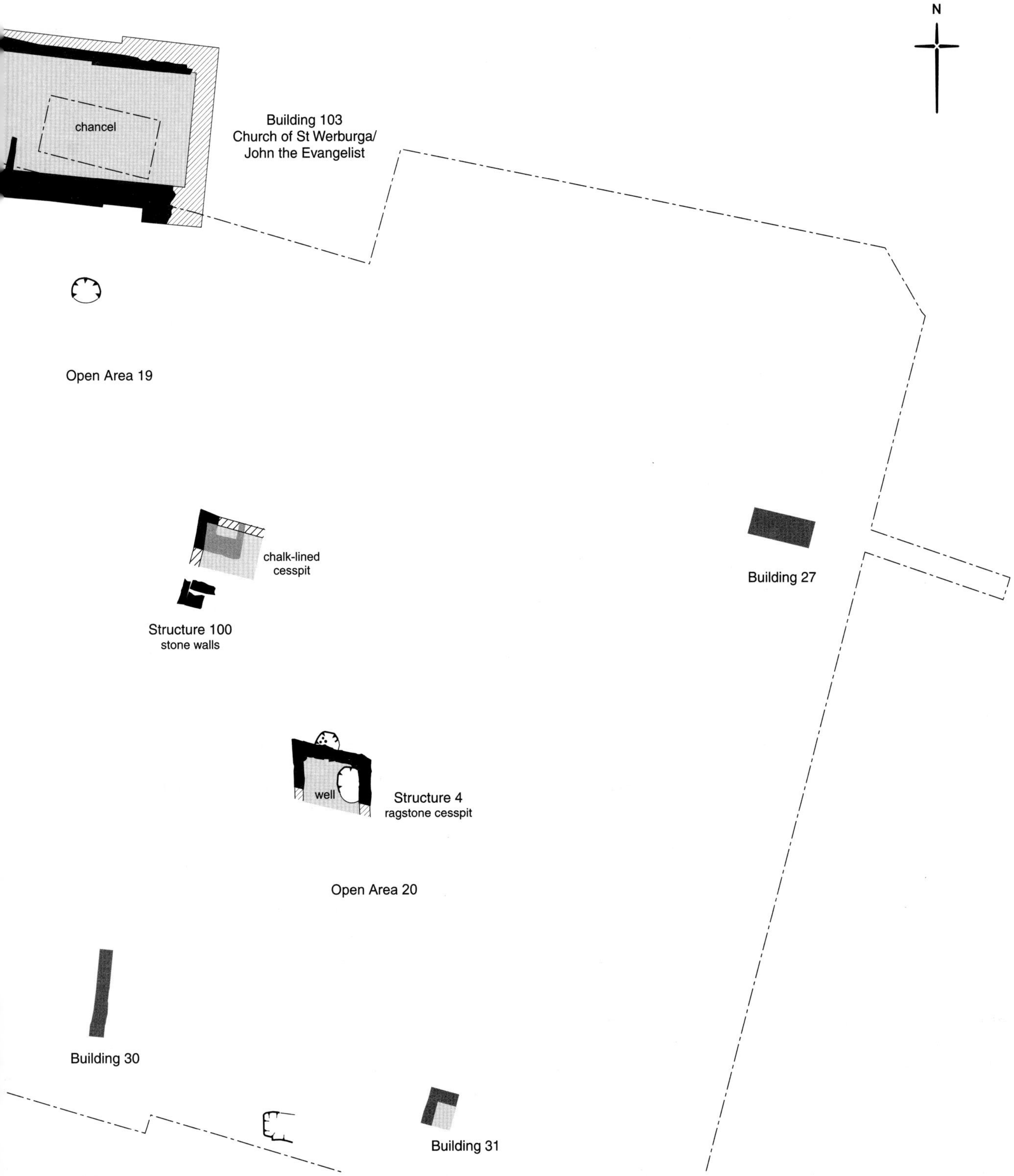

Building 34. This new orientation appears to be derived from that of Bread Street, rather than Friday Street, despite the fact that Open Area 19 and Structure 100 actually lie closer to the latter, and Structure 4 is equidistant from the two.

A number of the rubbish and cesspits, particularly Structure 3, produced finds assemblages indicative of a wealthy household or households in the area, including a number of pieces of imported glassware (see Fig 37). The range of pottery types differs from that of period 8, with Surrey Whitewares typical of the 14th and 15th centuries (Table 8). The presence of several near complete pots suggests that they derive from adjacent buildings, including a kitchen. The cesspits Structures 3 and 4, and one in Open Area 28, continued in use into the 16th and 17th centuries (see 2.11 below).

Fig 36 'Westminster' floor tile with a previously unknown design of a lion and probably a snake (1:2)

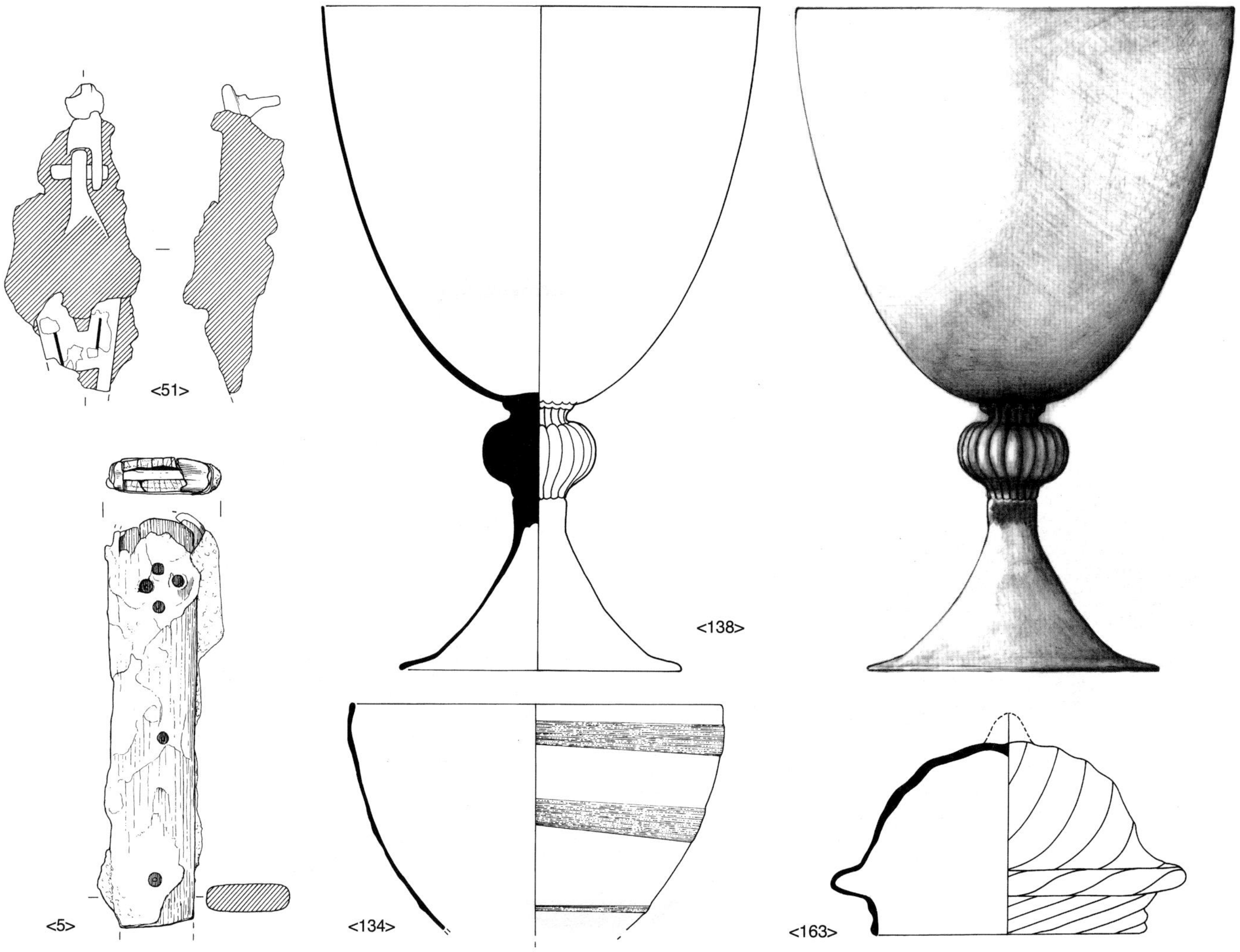

Fig 37 Finds from rubbish pits in Open Areas 27 and 28, and from cesspit Structure 3, periods 9 and 10: a copper-alloy suspension mount and corroded pendant, the latter with gilding <51>; a knife handle with wooden scales on either side of an iron tang, and a copper-alloy end cap, 15th or 16th century <5>; an imported very high-quality stemmed drinking vessel, possibly Italian, late 15th or 16th century <138>; an imported colourless glass drinking cup with applied trails of thin opaque white glass, probably from southern France, 14th or 15th century <134>; an imported mould-blown colourless glass lid with diagonal ribbing, possibly Venetian, 16th or 17th century, from the later use of Structure 3 in period 10 <163> (<51> and <5> 1:1, <138>, <134> and <163> 1:2)

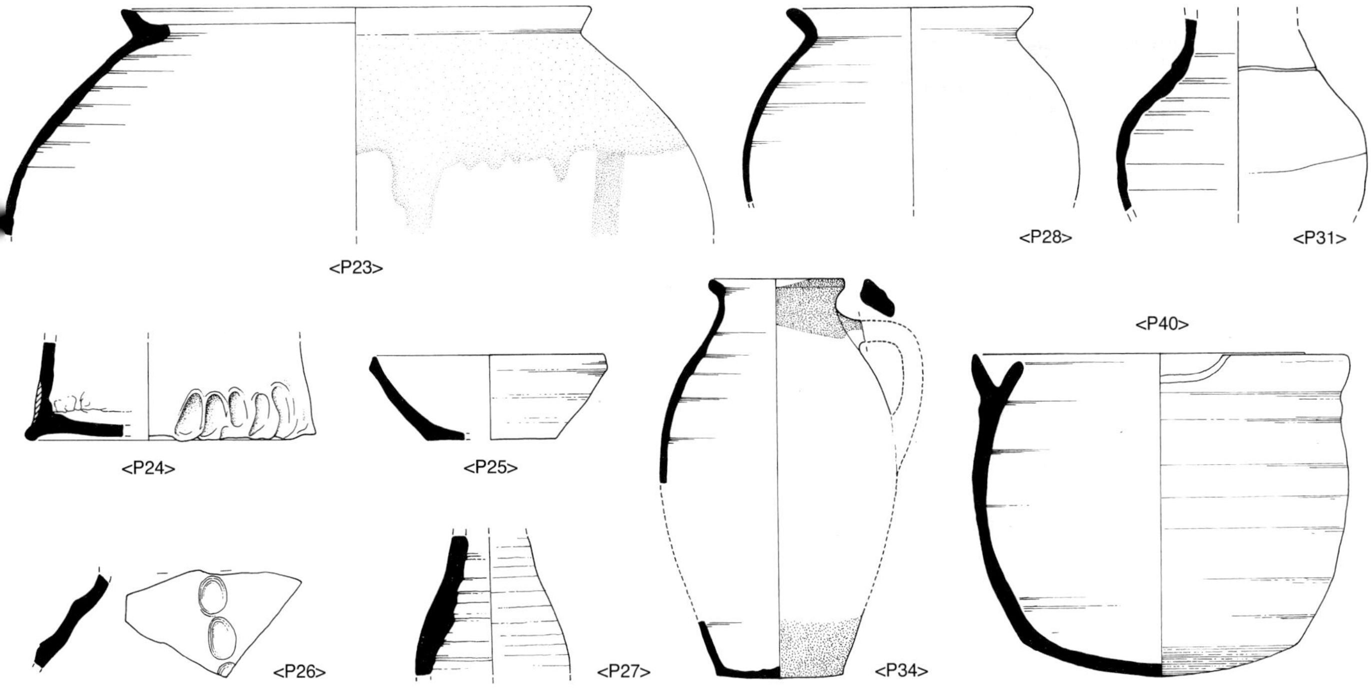

Fig 38 Pottery from the fills of pits in Open *Areas* 19, 27 and 28, and cesspit Structure 3, periods 9 and 10: Coarse Border ware bifid-rimmed cooking pot <P23>; Late Medieval Hertfordshire Glazed ware jug <P24>; Kingston-type ware dish <P25>; Calcareous Coarse London-type ware ? spouted pitcher <P26>; Coarse London-type ware bottle <P27>; Rhenish Greyware Kugeltopf <P28>; *a* crudely made Coarse Border ware jug with roughly knife-trimmed neck, white slip and patchy yellow glaze, apparently copying *a* Raeren Stoneware drinking jug <P31>; Early Border ware drinking jug <P34>; Post-medieval Redware distillation base <P40> (1:4)

Fig 39 Pottery from the fills of pits in Open *Areas* 27 and 28 (periods 9 and 10), cesspit Structure 3 (period 9), Structure 4 (period 9) and Structure 5 (period 10). Back row, from left to right: Early Post-medieval Redware distillation base (<P40>, S3); Siegburg Stoneware drinking jug (<P41>, S4); Kingston ware small rounded jug (<P30>, *OA*27); Early Border ware drinking jug and sherds (<P34>, *OA*28). Front row: Dutch Redware cooking pot with knife-cuts on the handle (<P36>, *OA*28); small Kingston ware dish (<P25>, *OA*27); Early Border ware money box (<P33>, *OA*28); Cheam ware money box with collared knop (<P42>, S5)

Fig 40 *View of slumped lining and relining of cesspit Structure 3, from the north-west (0.5m scale)*

Table 8 *Selected dating evidence, period 9 (1230–1440)*

Land use	Context	Evidence	Description	Sherds	Date range
OA19	[893]	pottery	CBW BIF; EBORD; KING; KING METCOP; LCOAR; LMHG; LOND BAL; LOND; LOND TULBAL; LOND HD; LOND NFR; SHER	165	1380–1500
OA27	[105]	pottery	KING; LCOAR; LOND BAL; LSS; SHER	13	1230–1300
OA27	[146]	pottery	EMS; EMSS; KING; KING HD; KING SMR; LCOAR; LOGR; LOND; LOND BAL; LOND HD; LOND NFR; LSS; MG; MISC; SHER; STAM	256	1310–50
OA28	[174]	pottery	KING; KING HD; LIMP; LOGR; LOND; LOND BAL; LOND EAS; LOND NFR; LOND ROU; MG; MGCOAR; SAIP; SHER	63	1340–1400
S3	[289]	pottery	CBW; CBW CIST; KING JUG; KING HD; LCOAR; LOND BAL; LOND NFR; MG JUG	75	1270–1300

2.11 Period 10: later medieval to Great Fire cellars and cesspits, 1440–1666

Five cellars, and presumably associated buildings, were constructed between the mid 15th century and the Great Fire of 1666 (Fig 41). Some of the pits in Open Area 28 continued in use, as did masonry-lined cesspits Structures 3 and 4, and three more masonry-lined pits were constructed.

Building 103: church of St John the Evangelist

A charnel pit containing pottery dated to c 1620 was found within the nave of the church, and probably represents clearance of burials immediately after the Great Fire, when the church was destroyed and not rebuilt (Schofield 1994, 106). Alternatively, exhumation might have taken place during repairs to the church in 1626 (Huelin 1996, 10).

Buildings 35, 36, 37 and 39

Evidence for Building 35 consisted of a poor-quality foundation of Kentish rag, Reigate stone and flint, aligned parallel to the church of St John the Evangelist. Building 35 was probably part of the cellar of a building fronting on to Friday Street, and may have been of early post-medieval date.

The only evidence for Building 36 was a heavily truncated section of foundation, or post pad, composed of chalk, Reigate stone and tile, oriented at an angle to the adjacent church and Building 35. Building 37 was a cellar wall constructed of chalk, tile, Kentish rag and Reigate stone, oriented parallel to Friday Street. Building 39 was comprised of a brick wall running north–south, bonded into a brick, chalk and Kentish rag wall running east–west, probably the corner of a cellar, or possibly a cesspit.

Building 38: large cellar; Open Area 31: pit

Open Area 31 is represented by a single large rubbish pit (not illustrated) dating to 1580–1700, that was cut by the construction of the cellar forming Building 38. The pit produced fragments of thin-walled glass bottles known as 'Betties' <131> and <132>. They were imported from Italy containing wine, and would have originally had wicker covers. These examples date to the 17th century. Part of a bulbous bottle <133> was also found, with a sloping neck and a simple out-turned rim, dating to the 16th/mid 17th century.

The pit was cut by the construction cut of a chalk-lined cellar, Building 38, more than 2.34m deep, which presumably lay beneath a building running back from Friday Street. Built into the western wall of the cellar was a small tin-glazed ointment pot, which dates to after 1580.

Open Area 29: pit; Open Area 30: cesspit reusing Roman wall

Open Area 29 is represented by a single rubbish pit, dated to between 1500 and 1800. A cesspit in Open Area 30 was constructed against the northern side of the southern wall of Roman Building 17, and crudely lined with Kentish rag rubble – probably reused Roman building material – to the north. The Roman wall, which must surely have been buried and unsuspected before the pit was dug, may well have been a fortuitous discovery on the part of the builder, who then used it as one side of the cesspit.

Structure 2: cesspit; Structure 5: cesspit; Structures 6 and 101: wells

Structure 2 was a large cesspit, lined with substantial chalk walls, probably constructed in the first half of the 16th century. It clearly went out of use after the Great Fire of 1666, its latest fill being burnt material dating to 1660–80 (Table 9).

Structure 5 consisted of a wall of chalk and Kentish rag, parallel to Friday Street, with a return comprised of Kentish rag and peg tile. This rather *ad hoc* construction was probably a cesspit lining, or possibly a rather badly built cellar, constructed after 1440.

Structure 6 was a well constructed of chalk, Kentish rag and pale yellow bricks. Structure 101 was probably a well, or possibly some form of soakaway or similar, with a brick and chalk lining, which rested on an oak ring, at the base of which was a wooden barrel filled with chalk chippings. The purpose of the latter is unknown; it was mostly filled with ash and coal waste, and was also backfilled after 1666.

Period discussion

The cellar walls of Buildings 35, 37, 38 and 39 imply new construction during this period, accompanied by wells and cesspits to serve the inhabitants of the buildings. Medieval Buildings 27, 30, 31, 33 and 34 may have continued in use from the preceding periods, and use of cesspits Structures 3 and 4 probably continued into the 16th century. One rubbish pit in Open Area 28 appears to have continued in use into the 17th century. While the orientations of Building 35 and cesspits Structures 2 and 5 reflected the reconstructed alignment of Friday Street, those of Buildings 37 and 38 were slightly different (see Fig 41), and this was also reflected in the unusual trapezoidal shape of cesspit Structure 4. It is possible that within the site boundaries the southern part of Friday Street actually curved slightly to the east. Pre-Fire maps show Friday Street variously as a straight line, or curving very slightly to the west, or east, at its southern end.

A make-up layer marking the disuse of cesspit Structure 3 (see 2.10 above) and dated to *c* 1500 contained an interesting assemblage of up to 15 vessels. The tablewares (cups and drinking jugs) are mainly of Early Border ware (see Fig 39), but also include Raeren Stoneware. Other forms comprise three money boxes and a base sherd from a rare Italian armorial vase (see 4.3 below). The coarsewares include a Cheam Whiteware bifid-rim cooking pot, and large dish and a jar with incised decoration of wavy lines, both in Early Post-medieval Redware. Also in this fabric is part of a distillation base which may have been used in metalworking rather than for domestic purposes (see Fig 38). A Raeren Stoneware spindlewhorl <43>, dating to *c* 1480–1550 or later, was intrusive in the fills of a pit from Open Area 28

Table 9 Selected dating evidence, period 10 (1440–1666)

Land use	Context	Evidence	Description	Sherds	Date range
B37 disuse	[62]	pottery	BORDG; PMFRB; PMR; TGW F	34	1670–90
S2	[66]	pottery	BORDG; BORDY; FREC jug; ITGW; PMBR; PMRE; PMSRG; TGW C	15	1630–50
S2 disuse	[59]	clay pipe			1660–80
S5	[283]	pottery	CBW; CHEA money box; CHEA BIF	85	1440–1500

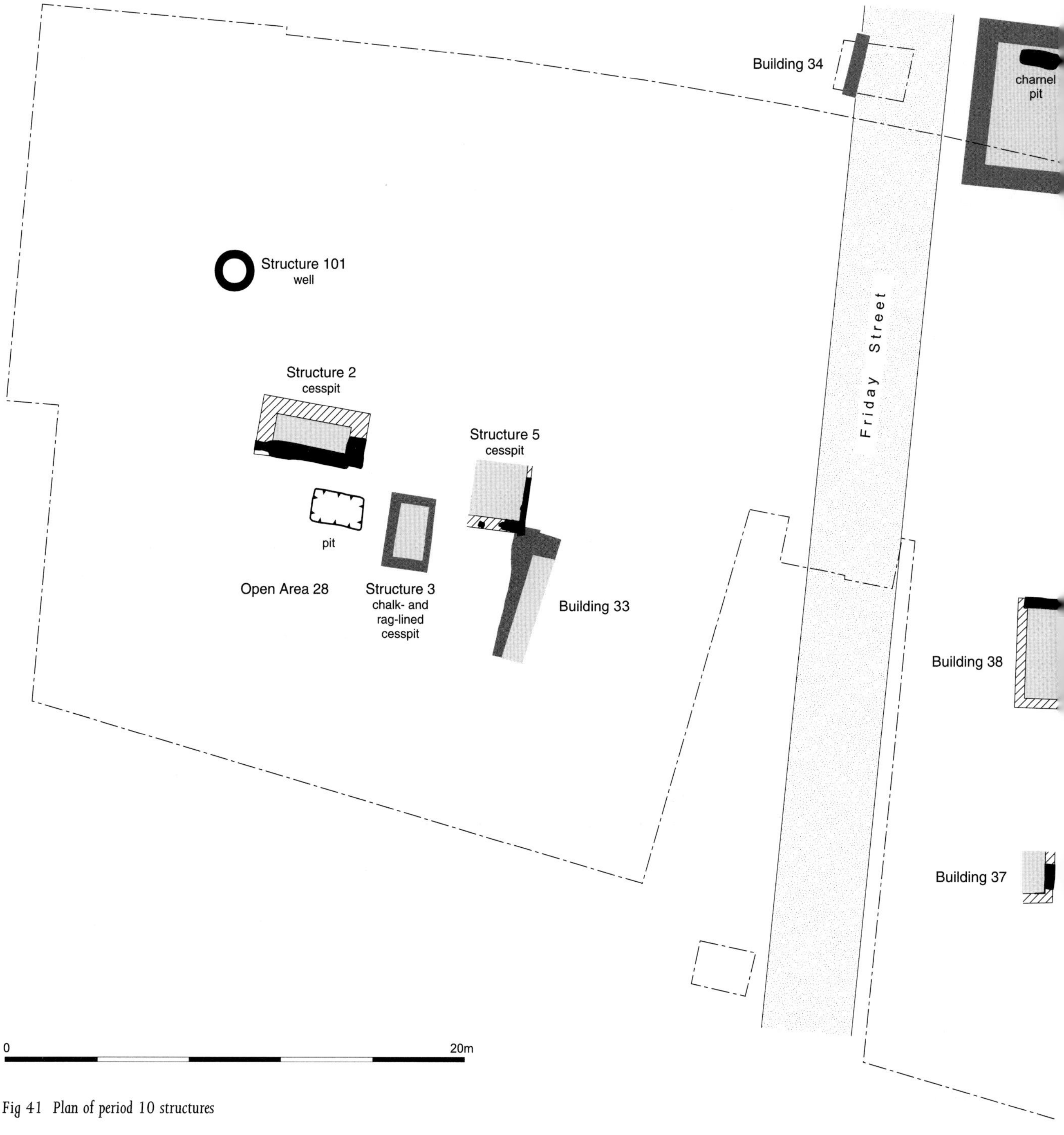

Fig 41 Plan of period 10 structures

in period 9. A rubbish pit in Open Area 28 produced part of an imported blue glass flagon <162> with an applied trail (17th century), and part of a fine mould-blown glass lid <163>, with diagonal ribbing, which may be Venetian (16th/17th century) (see Fig 37).

Leake's map of the destruction wrought by the Great Fire shows that the whole area of the site was razed, sweeping away the church and all of the surviving medieval and 16th- to 17th-century buildings.

2.12 Period 11: rebuilding after the Great Fire, 1666–*c* 1800

The church of St John the Evangelist was not rebuilt after the Great Fire, but the area of the church and churchyard to the south continued to be used as a burial ground. Brick buildings replaced those materials in use before the Great Fire (Fig 42).

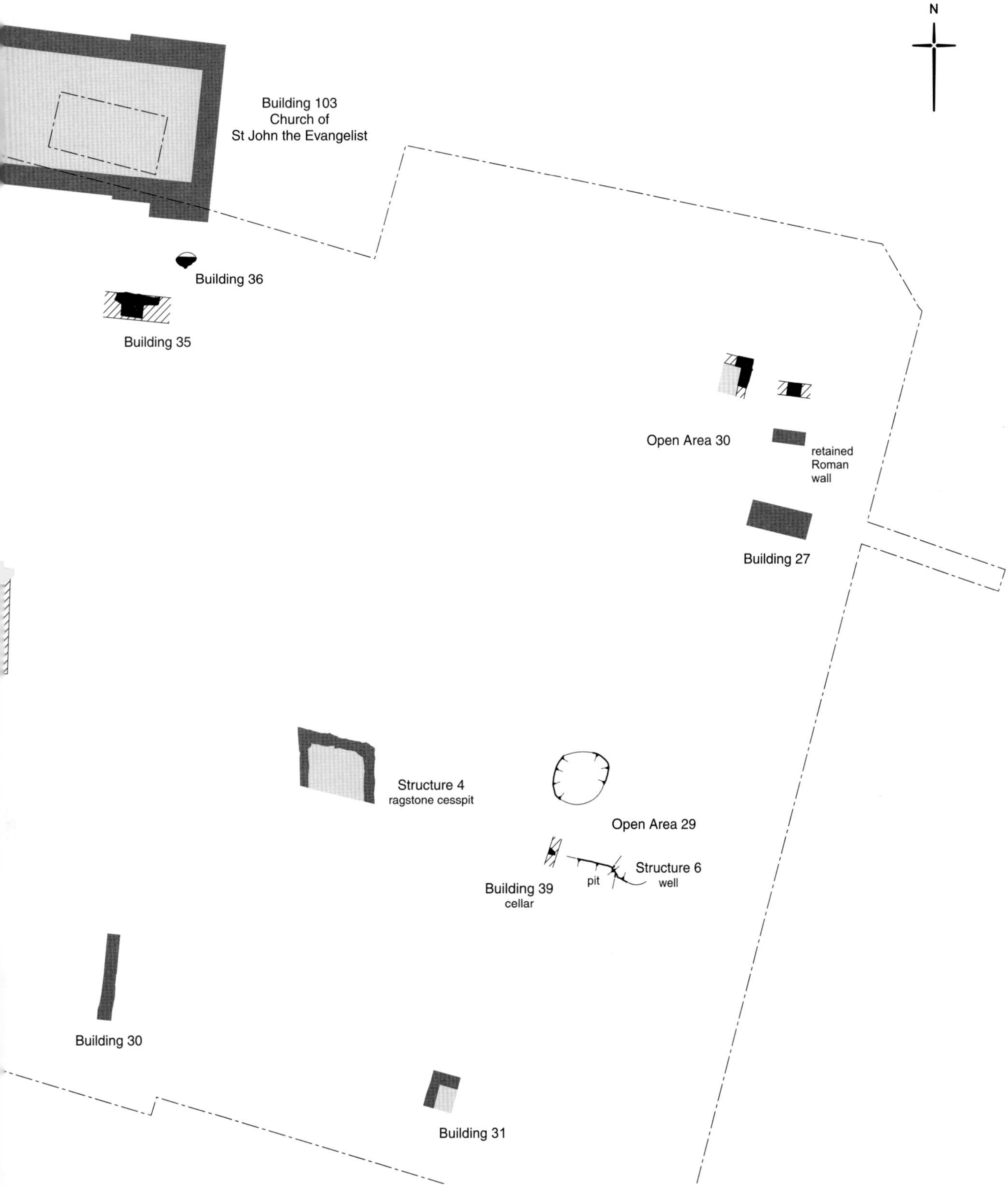

Structure 102: brick vault and burials

The use of the former churchyard as a burial ground was demonstrated by the eastern end of a brick and chalk vault, containing 18th-century coffins, as well as a second vault within the area of the former nave. This burial ground was used until the middle of the 19th century.

Building 34 rebuilt; Buildings 40 and 41: brick cellars

Rebuilding in brick after the Great Fire was demonstrated by a brick wall inserted into the medieval cellar of Building 34. Building 40 was a red and yellow brick cellar or cesspit. 'Building 41' records two cellars on either side of Friday

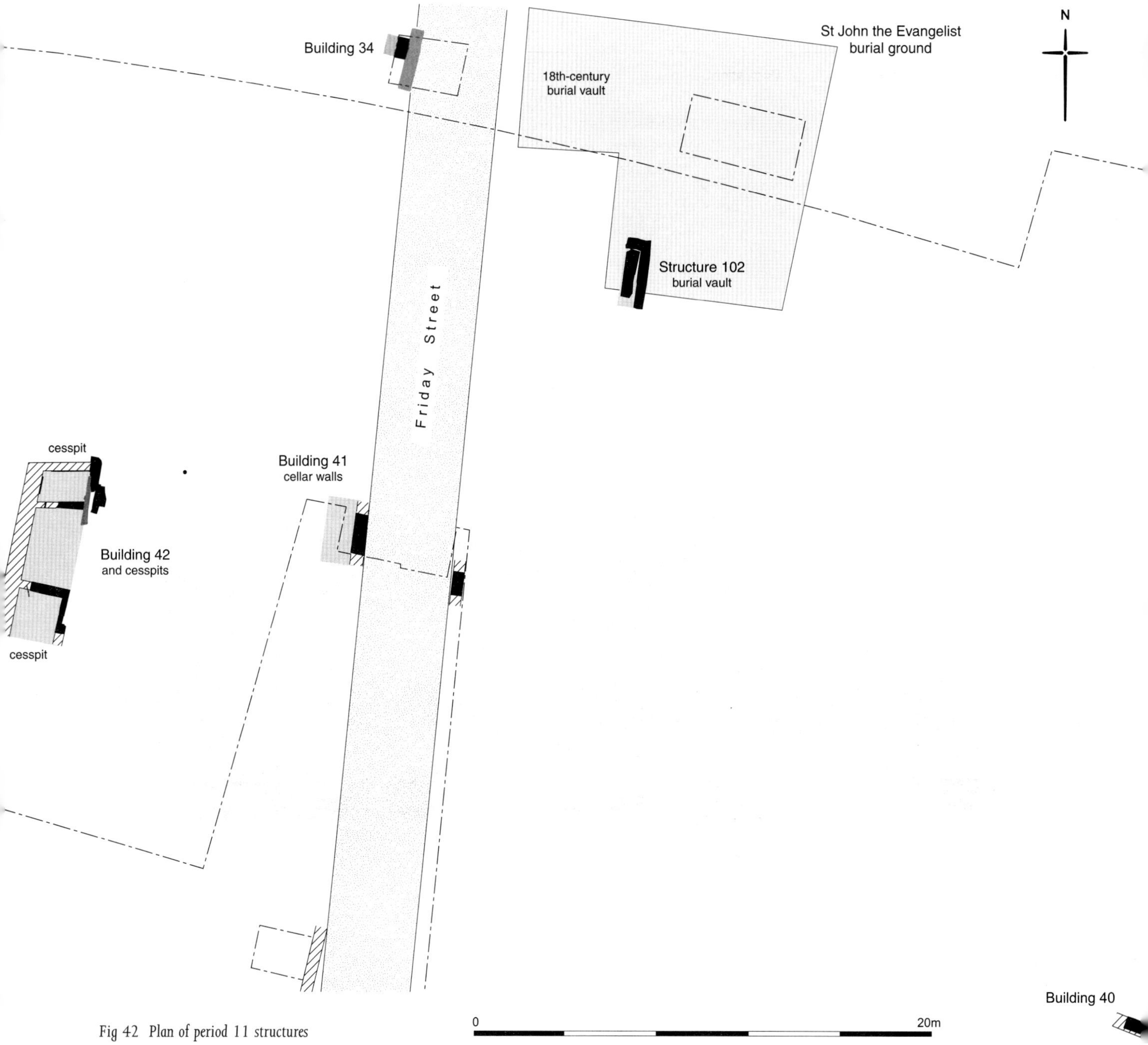

Fig 42 Plan of period 11 structures

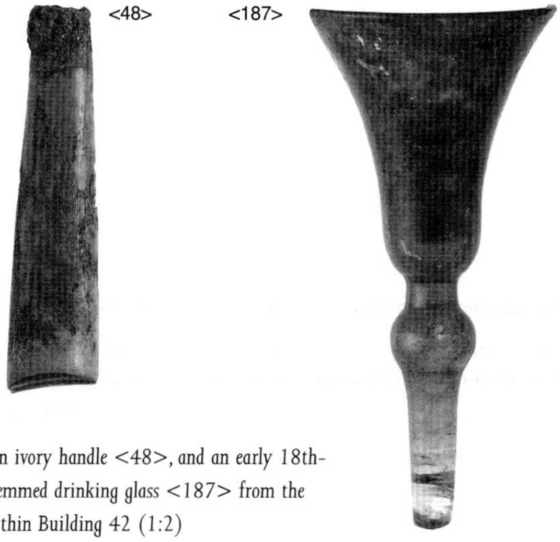

Fig 43 *An ivory handle <48>, and an early 18th-century stemmed drinking glass <187> from the cesspits within Building 42 (1:2)*

Street: that to the west was part of the 17th-century post-Fire reconstruction, but that to the east may have been later in date (Table 10).

Building 42: brick wall and cesspits

Building 42 consisted of a brick wall parallel with Friday Street, with two cesspits built against it. Probably the wall formed the back of the building, with the cesspits inside it, or possibly this was actually a boundary wall, with external cesspits built against it. The northern pit made use of the earlier masonry of Structure 5 (see 2.11 above) at its base. The southern pit included a soft yellow brick dating from the mid 14th to mid 15th centuries, which may be a Flemish import (Ryan 1996, 31–3).

Table 10 Selected dating evidence, period 11 (1666–c 1800)

Land use	Context	Evidence	Description	Sherds	Date range
B41	[33] and [35]	building material	3032		1666–1800
B42	[57]	pottery	BORDG CHP2; BORDY; CHPO; CREA; PMR; SWSG; TGW A; TGW C	117	1740–80
B42	[58]	pottery	CHPO BATV; CHPO BW; PMR; RBOR; RBORSL; SWSG; TGW plate FBJ floral decoration; TGW C; TGW D; WEST	42	1720–50
B42	[58]	clay pipes	AD26 <147>; AO18; AO20; AO22; AO25 <149> <153> <236> <241>; AO26 <145> <150> <151>; OS10; OS11 <146> <156> <220> <221> <233–5> <237–9> <242–5>; OS12 <148> <152> <154> <155> <222–32> <251> <152>		1730–60

Fig 44 Finds from the cesspits within Building 42. Back row, left to right: Creamware plate; plain white tin-glazed ware chamber pot and dish. Front row: Red Border ware dish with slip decoration; clay tobacco pipes of Atkinson and Oswald (1969) type 25 (with heel) and type 26 (with spur); Post-medieval Redware chamber pot; Westerwald Stoneware chamber pot; Post-medieval Redware handled bowl

Fig 45 18th-century biblical tin-glazed wall tile <21>, probably Dutch, from a cesspit within Building 42 (1:2)

The two cesspits produced a plain ivory handle <48>, probably 18th century in date, and an early 18th-century stemmed drinking glass with a bell-shaped bowl and solid inverted baluster stem <187> (Fig 43). A mixed group of 18th-century kitchenwares and tablewares was recovered, including vessels in Chinese porcelain and two chamber pots (Fig 44). One of the latter was whole, and had, no doubt, slipped from the hand of the person emptying it into the cesspit below.

A blue on white tin-glazed wall tile decorated with a biblical scene (Fig 45) was also found in one of these cesspits; it probably came from a decorative tiled area in a kitchen or from a fireplace surround <21>. The design and sandy clay fabric suggest that this is a Dutch import of the 18th century. The subject, the Mocking of Christ (Matthew 27:27–30; Mark 15:16–20), is an unusual one, as is the decorative treatment of the barred oxhead motifs in each corner. Van Sabben and

Hollem (1987, 111, fig 371) illustrate a Dutch tile with the same biblical scene and similar corner decoration, and another with almost identical barred oxhead corners.

Period discussion

The Ordnance Survey map of 1873 shows that post-Fire construction increased in density until the site was completely occupied by buildings, except for the tree-shaded burial ground and Friday Street. These structures were destroyed when the area suffered severe bomb damage in 1941, but post-war rebuilding did not commence until 1954, with the construction of a single office block on the site. This was Gateway House, bounded to the west by New Change, which runs through the site of what had previously been the block of buildings between Friday Street and Old Change, adjacent to St Paul's. The construction work provided the opportunity for the first archaeological investigation on the site.

3

Discussion and conclusions: topographical development from the Roman to medieval periods

3.1 Roman development

For the first five or ten years after the Roman conquest in AD 43 the site of 25 Cannon Street lay on the underutilised margins of the new city, and the first construction activity may not have taken place until AD 60. The first buildings in period 2, and possibly an alley, as well as the earlier phase of period 3, *c* AD 70–100, were laid out on parallel alignments, implying a degree of regularity and organisation in the process of construction. There was little evidence for the continuity of individual land divisions; only Buildings 8 and 9 in period 3 demonstrated the replacement of a building with one in the same position.

The construction of Building 10 in the later part of period 3, perhaps *c* AD 100, saw the introduction of a slightly different alignment in the eastern side of the site, reflected in a change in the orientation of the ditch in Open Area 9, and which extended across the northern side of the site during period 4. New buildings in the central part of the site, however, still respected the original alignment throughout periods 3 and 4. This change in alignment corresponded to that immediately to the east at Watling House (Shepherd 1986, 138–9), and lay parallel to that of the Flavian–Trajanic (AD 70–120) buildings at Watling Court (Perring and Roskams 1991, figs 29–30). It would appear that a phase of rebuilding on parallel alignments took place at this time, from Watling Court in the east across to Building 10 in the west. This orientation appeared to continue to the south of Watling House, and was mirrored by poorly dated buildings seen within Cannon Street (Lakin 1997, 12–13: second building) and at St Mildred Bread Street (Marsden et al 1975, 172–81).

It has been suggested from the layout of buildings and alleys at Watling Court that a Roman road might have run approximately along the line of modern Cannon Street (Perring and Roskams 1991, 115). Lakin (1997, 12) has noted the presence of two phases of Roman buildings beneath Cannon Street. These buildings appear to be continuations of those at Watling House, and strongly suggest that if a road existed, it must have lain to the south, and to the north of St Mildred Bread Street and the 'small Roman bath' at Cannon Street (Fig 46) (RCHME 1928, 111–12).

Rebuilding in the 2nd century at 25 Cannon Street and Watling House was originally interpreted as reconstruction after the Hadrianic fire (Shepherd 1986, 136–8). While the additional dating evidence from the recent excavations is not conclusive, it would now appear that the rebuilding took place earlier, corresponding to the construction at Watling Court in the half-century between the Boudican and Hadrianic fires (Perring and Roskams 1991, 29–30).

Evidence from the Watling Court excavations showed that the site developed from an underutilised area into one extensively built over by the late 1st century. The 1954 findings from the current site and Watling House reflected a similar pattern (Perring and Roskams 1991, 30, 115).This may have been the case at 25 Cannon Street, as demonstrated by the

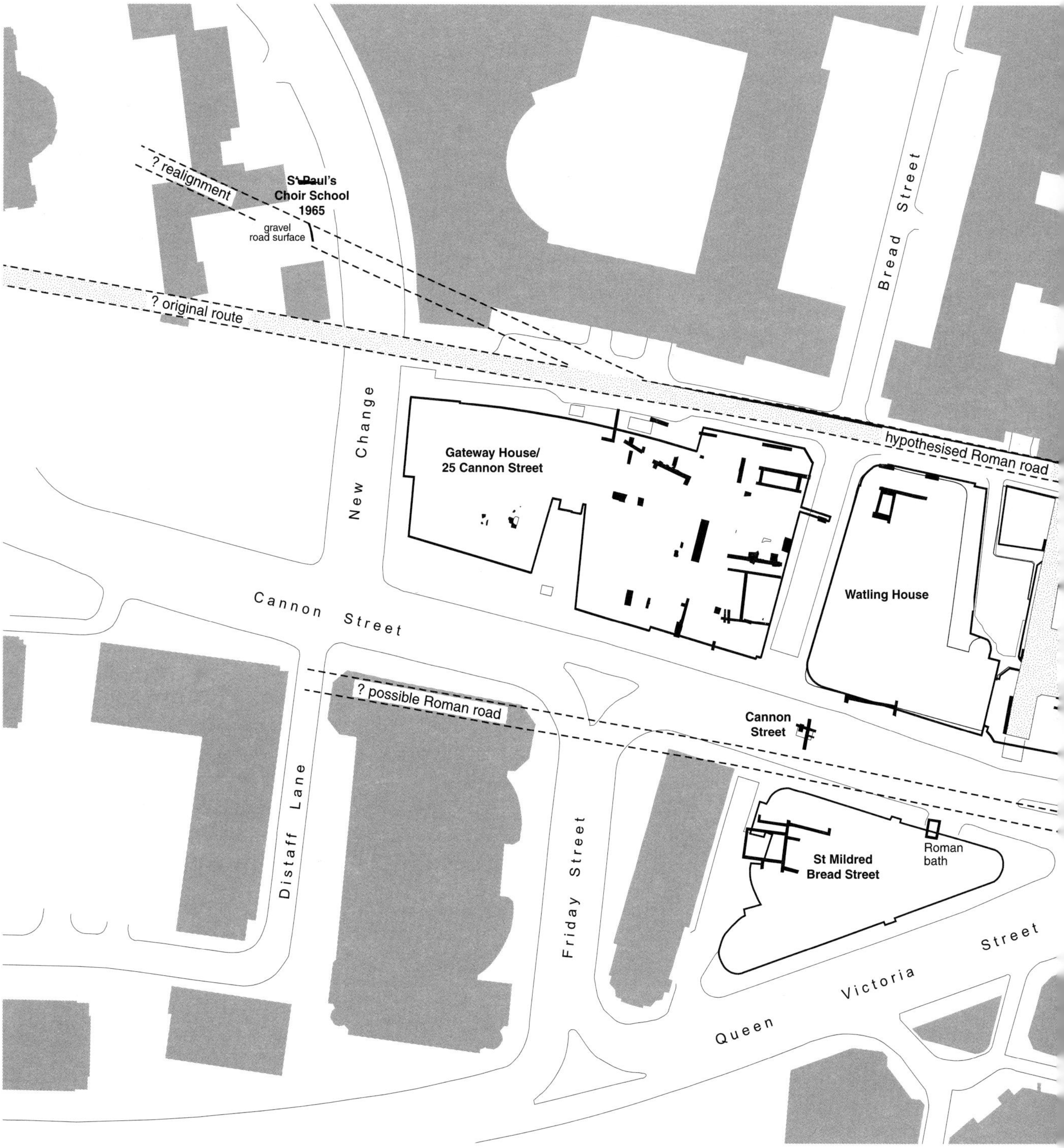

Fig 46 Plan showing hypothesised Roman roads in relation to the period 4 buildings, Building 20 in period 5, and buildings on other Roman sites in the vicinity

gradual encroachment of buildings upon Open Area 9 during period 3. In period 4 there may have been an extensive yard between Buildings 10 and 17, some 15m across (see Fig 15, around OA100), suggesting that there were still some open spaces within the insula.

Building 20 in period 5 marks the advent of a noticeably different alignment from the previous construction, probably in response to some major topographic influence, such as the realignment of a road.

Heavy truncation and preservation of a proportion of the site *in situ* prevent a reconstruction of much of the character of the occupation. Although there was some small amount of evidence for metalworking and antlerworking in the vicinity, the impression from the data is one of an area that was largely residential. The extensive 3rd- or 4th-century tessellated floors of Building 21 suggest moderately wealthy inhabitants; although the floors do not compare in quality with those seen at Watling Court or Milk Street (Perring and Roskams 1991, 90–4). They are, however, of notably better quality than those of the earlier Building 14/15.

It has been hypothesised that the economy and levels of occupation of Londinium declined in the late 2nd century

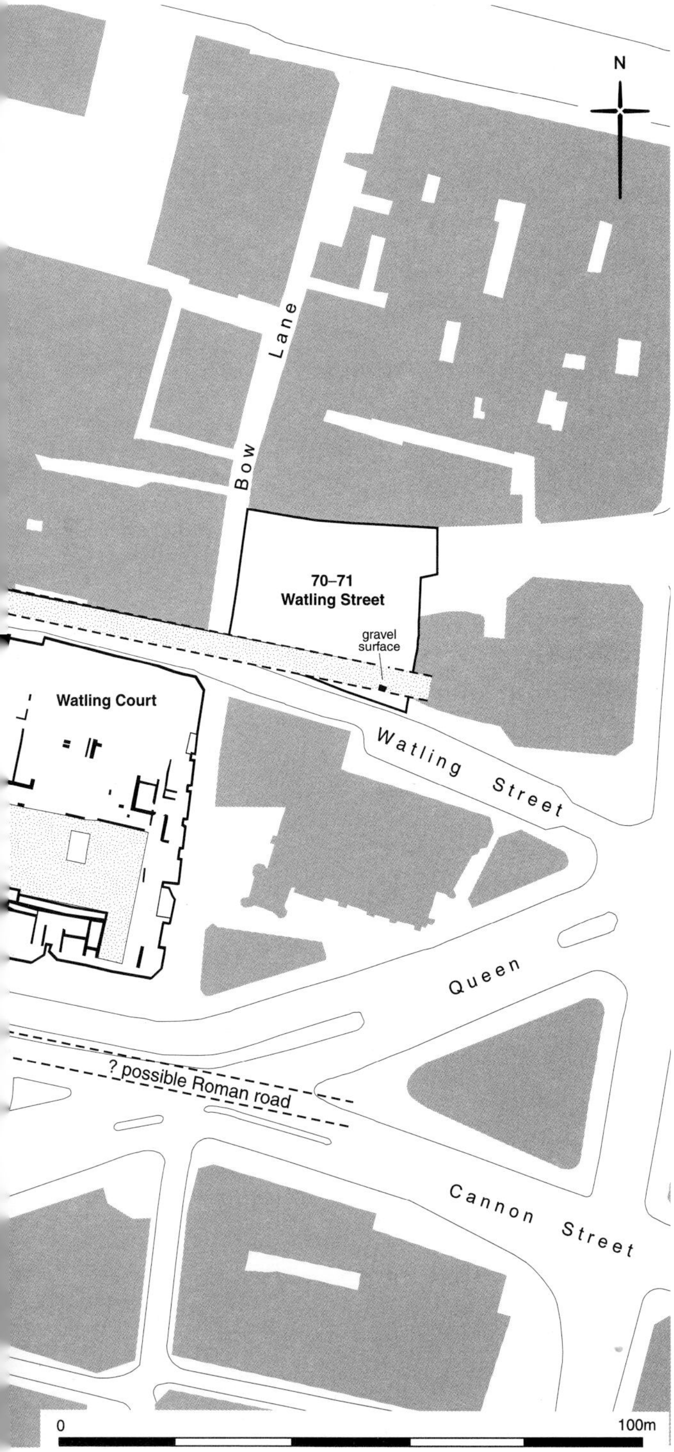

(Marsden and West 1992; Perring 1991, 76–8), and that this was reflected in a lack of 3rd- or 4th-century buildings at Watling Court and other sites (Perring and Roskams 1991, 44, 120). The recent work demonstrates that a large building (B21) was constructed after AD 250, and another masonry building (B20) after at least AD 200, so the conclusions for Watling Court clearly do not apply here. This must call into question whether other late Roman deposits had been truncated on the sites to the east. It is currently considered that such a decline was short-lived, and that recovery may have started by *c* AD 200; this may correspond with the dating of Buildings 20 and 21.

The 1954 observations at Watling House, immediately to the east of the present site, included a Neronian/early Flavian pit (*c* AD 55–70) containing an assemblage of glass fragments, discussed by John Shepherd (1986, 141–3). The material included furnace fragments and moils (waste glass from the end of the blowing iron), interpreted as coming from a glass workshop in the vicinity. The pit also contained glass cullet (waste fragments collected for recycling), which was notable for a lack of rims and bases (Shepherd 1986, 142).

The glass from the current site produced no evidence for furnace or production waste. Nor is there any indication that the material was intended for reprocessing at a glass workshop. The assemblage includes rim, body and base fragments, which occurred throughout the site, both spatially and stratigraphically. No groups of glass indicative of material that was specifically intended for recycling were found.

3.2 A Roman road to the north of the site?

The orientation of Buildings 10, 17 and 19, in periods 3 and 4 (*c* AD 100 or 140 to 250), was shared by those on the northern side of Watling House (? post-*c* AD 120), and by the period IV (*c* AD 70–120) buildings and alleys at Watling Court (see Fig 46). It has been suggested that these alignments reflected that of a Roman road running beneath modern Watling Street, which forms the northern boundary of the site (Shepherd 1986, 135–6, fig 13; Perring and Roskams 1991, 115).

In 1833 'a substratum of chalk ... paved with flint', and presumed to be a Roman road, was seen during the construction of a sewer in Watling Street (*Gentleman's Magazine* 1833, 422). Although this observation suggests that such a road did exist, it cannot be located precisely, and may have been situated some distance to the east. In addition, a section of early medieval chalk and gravel foundation could perhaps fit this description, while the depth of '20 feet' at which it was supposed to have been observed would place it below the surface of the natural terrace gravels.

The date at which this road may have originated remains obscure. Perring and Roskams (1991, 115) note that 'Flavian buildings immediately to the south fronted on to it'. This presumably refers to the buildings on the northern edges of 25 Cannon Street (B17 and B19) and Watling House, but does not actually correspond with Shepherd's phasing (1986, fig 11), nor with the post-AD 200 date for Building 17. The pottery dating Building 17 may, however, be intrusive (see 2.5 above). Conversely, although the Flavian buildings at Watling Court did not actually front on to this road, the orthogonal grid of alleys and buildings did respect it, which does support a date of *c* AD 70–120 (Perring and Roskams, figs 29–30 and 39).

The projection of Building 20 across the hypothesised route is thought to reflect a realignment of the road, which from the recent evidence may have taken place in the late 2nd or 3rd century. A section of road, 4.1m wide and 1.2m deep, was recorded during an excavation at St Paul's Choir School in 1965 (Marsden 1968, 3), and it has been suggested that this is part of the realigned road (Shepherd 1986, 135–6). The original alignment heads west towards a point some 11m to the north of (modern) Ludgate Hill, but the location of the Roman gate in that area is not known; the realignment points in the general direction of Newgate.

The precise alignment of the hypothesised road cannot be ascertained from the available data; previous reconstructions have used the Roman walls at the northern edge of the site and at Watling House as a possible southern boundary for the road, yet these might have been internal walls. The combined information from both 1954 and the recent excavations shows a certain symmetry between the southern side of Building 19 and the northern side of Building 10 (see Fig 15). This suggests the possibility that Buildings 17 and 19 continued north of the site boundaries. If this were so, then the road would lie some 5m further north than the position suggested by Shepherd (1986, fig 13) and Perring and Roskams (1991, fig 93 'Road 12'). The realigned route suggested in Fig 46 has been constructed from the orientation of the southern wall of Building 20, projected to the north-west from the location of the northern wall of that building. While this remains only a possibility, it has the virtue that, if the realigned road did bend to correspond to Building 20, and was consistently *c* 4.1m wide, it would cross the recorded location at St Paul's Choir School.

A recent observation of a 0.35m deep Roman gravel surface at 70–71 Watling Street, 120m to the east of the present site, lay 1.4m to the north of modern Watling Street (Bowsher 1999, 15, fig 3). This lies at a point where it might correspond to either an eastward extension of the alignment suggested by Shepherd, or that suggested above, but not that of Perring and Roskams, which turns to the south-east at a point immediately east of Watling Court, and thus passes to the south of this new observation. This, however, may not be a road, but an alley or yard; it was only 0.35m deep compared with the 1.2m seen at St Paul's Choir School, and *c* 1.6m at Well Court (Perring and Roskams 1991, fig 48).

3.3 Saxon and medieval development

While it is not impossible that some walls from the Roman buildings were standing above ground level into the Late Saxon and early medieval periods, none of the period 7 buildings were aligned with later Roman structures in periods 4 and 5.

Fig 47 The new development at 25 Cannon Street

In particular, the cellars of Buildings 23 and 24 had very clearly been dug through Roman buildings, without respecting their alignments.

The Saxo-Norman buildings of period 7 exhibited two slightly different alignments. Building 23, built 1050–1100, and Building 24 lay parallel to modern Bread Street, and presumably to Saxon and medieval Bread Street. This is unsurprising, as Bread Street, or at least its southern end, is documented from the 9th century (see 2.8 'Period discussion' above), but this supports the theory that the northern half was also in existence by the early 11th century, more than a century before the second reference to Bread Street. Modern Bread Street overlies the Roman Buildings 16 and 21, and the subsequent 'dark earth', demonstrating the trend for Saxon streets to disregard the earlier Roman alignments (Schofield et al 1990, 153).

None of the Saxo-Norman buildings reflected the reconstructed alignment of Friday Street, although Building 23 lay closer to Bread Street and might not be expected to. This implies that Friday Street was not constructed until after Buildings 22, 24 and 25 had been built, probably in the first half of the 11th century. The road was presumably in existence by the time that the church of St Werburga was established, between 1098 and 1108, which also differed in alignment from the Saxo-Norman buildings. Taken together, these suggest a date in the second half of the 11th century for the construction of Friday Street, which corresponds with that of the earliest pottery recovered from the road gravels (see 2.9 above).

The church of St Werburga and the adjacent Building 32 shared an east–west alignment that probably reflected that of medieval Aethelingestraete/Watling Street. This differed from the orientations displayed by Roman buildings, albeit only slightly from that of Buildings 17 and 19. In addition, the alignment of the northern side of Buildings 17 and 19, even if reconstructed further to the north (see 3.2 above), would not align with the northern wall of the church. This implies that there was little continuity, perhaps none, between medieval Watling Street and a Roman precursor.

The medieval roads to the south of the site were Distaff Lane to the west of Friday Street, understood to have been in use by the 12th century (Lobel 1989, 72), and between Friday Street and Basing Lane an alley or road which went by various names, ending as Little Friday Street. These roads were subsumed into the much wider Cannon Street in 1852, but would appear from 17th- and 18th-century maps to have had similar orientations. Because of the widening of Cannon Street, the medieval street frontages and buildings along them fall outside the limits of 25 Cannon Street.

Despite the loss of the alignments of the medieval and later building plots within the site, the outline of the new development echoes the lines of the medieval streets: Friday Street as a pedestrian route beneath its portico (Fig 47), and along Bread Street and Watling Street. The new building is the heir to two millennia of construction and occupation at 25 Cannon Street, and finds from the excavations will be displayed within it.

4

Specialist appendices

Full catalogues and supporting information on the finds and environmental remains would be too lengthy to present in this publication, and are available in the site archive.

4.1 Roman pottery codes

Robin Symonds

Table 11 Roman pottery fabric codes

Code	Description	Date range
Amphorae		
BAETE	Baetican Dressel 20/Haltern 70 amphora fabric, early	50–170
CAT	Catalan Dressel 2–4 amphora fabric	50–150
GAUL1	Pélichet 47/Dressel 30 amphora fabric (Peacock & Williams 1986, 27/30)	50–250
GAUL2	London-type 555/Haltern 70 *similis* amphora fabric	50–120
RHOD	Rhodian amphora fabric	50–150
Samian wares		
SAMCG	Central Gaulish samian ware	120–250
SAMEG	East Gaulish samian ware	150–300
SAMLG	La Graufesenque samian ware	50–100
Imported fine wares		
CGBL	Central Gaulish/Lezoux Black Colour-coated ware	150–250
KOLN	Cologne Colour-coated ware	100–40
LYON	Lyon Colour-coated ware	50–70
MOSL	Moselkeramik	200–75
Romano-British fine wares		
EGGS	Miscellaneous eggshell ware	70–120
MHAD	Much Hadham ware	200–400
NVCC	Nene Valley Colour-coated ware	150–400
OXRC	Oxfordshire Red/Brown Colour-coated ware	270–400
OXWC	Oxfordshire White Colour-coated ware	240–400
RDBK	?Verulamium Region 'ring and dot' beaker fabric	50–100
Black-burnished-type wares		
BB1	Black-burnished 1 ware	120–400
BB2	Black-burnished 2 ware	120–250
BB2F	Black-burnished 2 ware with fine fabric	140–250
BBS	Black-burnished-style ware	120–400
Fine reduced wares		
FINE	Miscellaneous fine ware	50–400
FMIC	Fine Micaceous Black/Grey ware	50–120
TN	Terra nigra	40–80
Reduced wares		
AHFA	Alice Holt/Farnham ware	250–400
AHSU	Alice Holt/Surrey ware	50–160
ERMS	Early Roman Micaceous Sandy ware	50–100
ERSB	Early Roman Sandy ware, B	60–120
HWC	Highgate 'C' Sand-tempered ware	70–160
SAND	Miscellaneous sand-tempered ware	50–400
Tempered wares		
COAR	Miscellaneous coarse ware	40–400
FLIN	Miscellaneous flint-tempered ware	50–200
GROG	Grog-tempered ware	40–400
HWB	Highgate 'B' Grog-tempered ware	40–100
HWBR	Highgate 'B' Red-slipped ware	40–100

Table 11 cont

Oxidised wares		
BHWS	Brockley Hill White slip	50–160
ECCW	Eccles ware	50–100
HOO	Hoo ware	50–100
LOXI	Local Oxidised ware	90–160
OXID	Miscellaneous oxidised ware	50–400
OXWS	Oxfordshire White-slipped Red ware	240–400
OXWW	Oxfordshire White ware	180–400
PORD	Portchester 'D' ware	350–400
RWS	Miscellaneous red- and white-slipped ware	50–300
VCWS	?Verulamium Region Coarse White-slipped ware	70–200
VRW	Verulamium Region White ware	50–160
Miscellaneous wares		
CC	Miscellaneous colour-coated wares	50–400

Table 12 Roman pottery form codes

Code	Description	Date range
1	Miscellaneous or otherwise unidentifiable flagon	50–400
1A	Collared (or Hofheim-type) flagon	50–100
1B7–9	Cup-mouthed ring-necked flagon (Marsh & Tyers 1978, fig 232.7–9)	140–200
2	Miscellaneous or otherwise unidentifiable jar	40–400
2A	Bead-rim jar	40–100
2A17	Black-burnished-type bead-rim jar (Marsh & Tyers 1978, fig 234.17)	120–200
2B	Short-necked jar	50–100
2D	Round-bodied necked jar with 'figure 7' rim	60–160
2E	Round-bodied necked jar with burnished shoulder	100–60
2F	Black-burnished-type everted-rim jar	120–250
2FX	Late AHFA version of 2F	250–400
2V	Storage jar	50–400
3	Miscellaneous or otherwise unidentifiable beaker	50–400
3B	Ovoid beaker	55–100
3C	Everted-rim beaker	50–100
3F4	'Poppyhead' beaker with short rim and low shoulder, usually has cordon below rim	100–60
4	Miscellaneous or otherwise unidentifiable bowl	40–400
4/5	Bowl/dish	50–400
4DR29	Dragendorff form 29 bowl	50–120
4DR37	Dragendorff form 37 bowl	70–400
4DR38	Dragendorff form 38 bowl	150–400
4F	Bowl with flat, hooked or folded-over rim	60–160
4H	Rounded-rim Black-burnished-type bowl	120–300
4M	Black-burnished-type flanged bowl	250–400
4P24	Young form 24 bowl	240–400
4RT12	Ritterling form 12 bowl	50–80
5	Miscellaneous or otherwise unidentifiable plate	50–400
5A	Plate with plain exterior profile	50–100
5J	Dish with simple rim	50–400
6	Miscellaneous or otherwise unidentifiable cup	50–400
6A	Copy of Dragendorff form 27 cup	50–120
6DR27	Dragendorff form 27 cup	50–160
6DR33	Dragendorff form 33 cup	70–200
6H	Hemispherical cup (Lyon/ n Italian)	50–100
7	Miscellaneous or otherwise unidentifiable mortarium	50–400
7HOF	Hooked-flange mortarium	50–140
7M22	Young type M22 mortarium	240–400
8	Miscellaneous amphorae	50–400
81J	Romano-British flat-bottomed amphora	50–100
8DR2–4	Dressel form 2–4 amphora	50–150
8DR20PW7	Dressel form 20 amphora (Peacock & Williams 1986, fig 65.7)	45–400
8G	Pélichet 47/ Dressel form 30/Gauloise type amphora	50–250
8G5	Gauloise type 5 amphora	50–250
9A	Lid (usually post-70)	50–400
9C	Tazza	50–250

Table 13 Roman pottery decoration codes

Code	Description	Date range
AL	Black-burnished-type acute-lattice decoration	120–250
ARCX	Arcs on later Black-burnished ware forms	250–400
BDD	Barbotine dot decoration	50–400
BR	Bead rim	40–400
BRD	Ring-and-dot barbotine decoration	50–400
BUD	Burnished decoration	50–400
DEC	Moulded decoration	50–400
HPOF	Post-firing hole(s)	50–400
HPRF	Pre-firing hole(s)	50–400
NCD	Incised decoration	50–400
OAL	Open acute-lattice decoration	140–300
OL	Obtuse-lattice decoration	250–400
RCD1	Sand/quartz roughcast decoration	50–120
RCD2	Clay pellet/grog roughcast decoration	50–300
RLD	Rilled decoration	50–400
ROD	Rouletted decoration	50–400
RPD	Red-painted decoration	50–400
SL	Single lattice	140–200
WBAD	White barbotine decoration	180–300
WL	Wavy line decoration	50–250

4.2 Late Saxon/medieval and later pottery codes

Lyn Blackmore

Table 14 Late Saxon/medieval pottery fabric codes

Code	Description	Date range
CBW	Coarse Border ware	1270–1500
CBW BIF	Cooking pots with bifid rim	1380–1500
CBW CIST	Cisterns	1340–1500
CHEA	Cheam Whiteware	1350–1500
CHEA BIF	Cooking pots with bifid rim	1440–1500
EMCH	Early Medieval Chalky ware	1050–1150
EMGR	Early Medieval Grog-tempered ware	1050–1150
EMIS	Early Medieval Iron-rich Sandy ware	1050–1150
EMS	Early Medieval Sandy ware	970–1100
EMSH	Early Medieval Shell-tempered ware	1050–1150
EMSS	Early Medieval Sand-and-shell-tempered ware	1000–1150
ESUR	Early Surrey ware	1050–1150
KING	Kingston-type ware	1230–1400
KING HD	Highly decorated (applied)	1230–1300
KING METCOP	Metal-copy baluster jug	1270–1350
KING SMR	Small rounded jug	1310–1400
LCALC	Calcareous London-type ware	1080–1200
LCOAR	Coarse London-type ware	1080–1200
LCOAR CALC	Calcareous LCOAR	1080–1200
LCOAR SHEL	Shelly Coarse London-type ware	1080–1200
LIMP	Limpsfield-type ware	1150–1300
LMHG	Late Medieval Hertfordshire Green-glazed ware	1340–1450
LOGR	Local Greyware	1050–1150
LOND	London-type ware	1080–1350
LOND BAL	London-type ware baluster	1080–1350
LOND EAS	London-type ware Early Style	1140–1200
LOND HD	London-type ware highly decorated (inc anthro/zoo)	1240–1350
LOND NFR	London-type ware North French Style	?1180–1270
LOND ROU	London-type ware Rouen Style	1180–1270
LOND TULBAL	London-type ware tulip-shaped baluster jug	1270–1350
LSS	Late Saxon Shelly ware	900–1050

Table 14 cont

MG	Mill Green ware	1270–1350
MGCOAR	Mill Green Coarse ware	1270–1500
MISC	Miscellaneous unidentified wares	900–1500
NEOT	St Neots ware	970–1100
NFRY	Miscellaneous North French Glazed ware	900–1200
REDP OLV	Red-painted ware – olive fabric	900–1250
SAIP	Saintonge Polychrome ware	1280–1350
SATH	Sandy Thetford-type ware	1000–1150
SHER	S Herts/Limpsfield Greyware	1140–1300
SSW	Shelly Sandy ware	1140–1220
STAM	Stamford ware	1050–1150
THET	Ipswich Thetford-type ware	900–1100

Table 15 Post-medieval pottery fabric codes

Code	Description	Date range
BORDG	Green-glazed Border ware	1550–1700
BORDG CHP2	Type 2 chamber pot	1650–1700
BORDY	Yellow-glazed Border ware	1550–1700
CHPO	Chinese porcelain	1580–1900
CHPO BATV	Batavian ware	1700–50
CHPO BW	Blue and white Chinese export porcelain	1590–1900
CREA	Creamware	1740–1880
EBORD	Early Border ware	1480–1550
FREC	Frechen Stoneware	1550–1700
ITGW	Italian Tin-glazed ware	1480–1800
PMBR	Post-medieval Bichrome Redware	1480–1600
PMFRB	Post-medieval Fine Redware with brown glaze	1580–1700
PMR	Post-medieval Redware	1580–1900
PMRE	Early Post-medieval Redware	1480–1600
PMSRG	Post-medieval Slip-coated Redware with green glaze	1480–1650
RBOR	Red Border ware	1580–1800
RBORSL	Red Border ware with slip-trailed decoration	1580–1800
SWSG	Staffs White Salt-glazed Stoneware	1720–80
TGW	English Tin-glazed ware	1570–1800
TGW A	Orton A (lead gl ext/Wan Li/blue/yellow)	1612–50
TGW C	Orton C (plain white gl)	1630–1800
TGW D	Orton D (lead gl ext/poly)	1630–80
TGW F	Orton F ('chinamen in grasses')	1670–90
WEST	Westerwald-type Stoneware	1590–1800

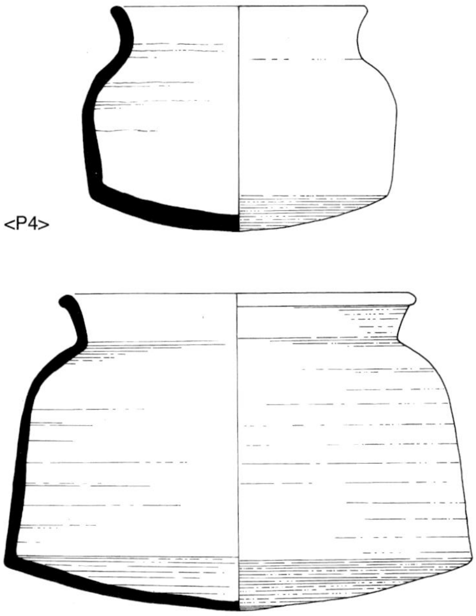

Fig 48 Two complete pots <P4> <P5> found buried beneath the floor of Building 23 (1:4)

4.3 Late Saxon/medieval and later pottery summary

Lyn Blackmore

The medieval and later pottery assemblage from the 1996–9 excavation comprises 2788 sherds. Late Saxon and medieval wares dominate (2292 sherds), with some 50 different medieval fabric types; three fabrics from early contexts could possibly be of 8th- or 9th-century date. Post-medieval wares amount to 495 sherds. In addition there is an extensive collection of finds from the 1954 excavations. Most sherds from both phases of excavation are quite large, and there are a number of near complete vessels.

Most of the Late Saxon/early medieval pottery comprises cooking pots and dishes which have been used in, or compare well with, the type series established for London (Vince and Jenner 1991, nos 223, 245, 291). In addition to the two complete pots (Fig 48; and see Figs 27–8) there are a few other complete and/or unusual forms (see Fig 29).

The medieval pottery (see Figs 34, 38–9) is dominated by jugs and cooking pots (see also Pearce et al 1985, nos 63, 98; Pearce and Vince 1988, nos 444, 448), but includes part of a curfew (<P21> Blackmore in prep) and a bottle-shaped pot in Coarse London-type ware (<P27> possibly an industrial vessel). The 13th–15th-century wares also include a dish, costrels and money boxes (Pearce and Vince 1988, nos 583, 588), and an extremely crudely made Coarse Border ware jug which appears to be copying a Raeren Stoneware drinking jug <P31>.

Medieval imports are not abundant in the finds from the site, but they are of significance for their range and generally early date (10th to 12th centuries). Later types include Saintonge Polychrome, Siegburg Stoneware (jakobakanne type and *Trichterhalsbecher*) and Dutch Redware, the latter including a good group of 11 pipkins and cauldrons from a single feature in Open Area 28 (see 2.10 above; cf Hurst et al 1986, 130–5, nos 178–82; Blackmore 1994, 37, fig 2 no. 11). One of these is of interest as it has a series of parallel knife-cuts across the base of the handle, possibly an owner's mark (see Fig 39).

The post-medieval wares (31 fabric variations) fall into three main groups dating to *c* 1480–1500/1550, 1580–*c* 1600, and the later 17th–18th centuries. Tin-glazed wares are most common by sherd-count; these include a small jar or albarello (for ointments or drugs). Redwares are the next most common; the latter include part of a distillation base with bifid rim (see Fig 38), internal glaze and external ferrous deposit (cf Moorhouse 1972, 111–13, fig 21). Whitewares are less common, but include a money box and a small jug (<P34>: see Figs 38–9); a rare find is part of a small whiteware cup, the handle of which is of red clay. The largest groups from the site are from rubbish pit group 108.24 in Open Area 28, period 9 (four boxes, 249 sherds), and cesspit group 111.69 from Building 42, period 11 (116 sherds). The latter includes some near complete chamber pots, bowls and plates (see Fig 44). Most of the imports date to *c* 1480–1550 and derive from Germany and the Low Countries, but part of a rare Italian armorial vase is also present <P39>; this is a high-status form which is shown in contemporary manuscripts; it probably relates to the Italian wares noted below. Frechen Stonewares are noticeably absent but a complete Westerwald Stoneware chamber pot was found.

A large amount of tin-glazed ware was found in the excavations of 1954, mostly from ER 166A (ER: Guildhall Museum Excavation Register entry), which contained many drug jars and ointment pots (now in the Museum of London reserve collections). An extremely rare and important find from ER 166D comprises sherds from at least one writing set, a small dish or inkwell, and part of a sander. Some of the Border wares have been published in the recent corpus (Pearce 1992, nos 46, 155, 312, 421). Also of note is an alembic found in a well (ER 191B, dated to 1580–1630). The stonewares include some high-quality pieces, notably two bellarmines with large and/or multiple medallions (ER 153 and ER 207).

One of the most significant groups is ER 161 (the fill of a cellar/garderobe), on which an extensive illustrated note has been published by Blake (1999, 45, *passim*). This contained several near complete pieces, including a mature Valencian Lustreware pedestal jug (Hurst 1977, no. 39; Blackmore 1994, col pl 3d) and three Italian jugs and vases. The latter comprise a large strap-handled jug and two smaller vases with arched handles; one bears the sacred 'IHS' monogram in blue and white, the other has polychrome floral decoration (Blake 1999, *passim*, fig 2.3 no. 8; see also Noël Hume 1977, 9, pl 3; Britton 1987, 99, no. 3; Hughes and Gaimster 1999).

Fuller details of these finds are available in the pottery archive, which comprises a fuller discussion of the wares and their distribution on the site, and notes on the 1954 finds.

4.4 Roman tile markings

Ian M Betts

A partial procuratorial stamp is impressed on an imbrex roofing tile <184> and a brick <181> (fabric group 2815) (Fig 49). Both have the same stamp (die 2A) which if complete would have read PPBRILON, interpreted as: P(rocuratores) p(rovinciae) Bri(tanniae) Lon(dini) 'The procurators of the province of Britain at London'. These were not *in situ*, but almost certainly derived from public buildings during the period AD 70–125, or from an official brickyard. Tiles impressed with this stamp were used in the public baths at Huggin Hill, the basilica, the amphitheatre and in a large building complex beneath Cannon Street Station and streets to the east: the so-called 'Governor's Palace' (Betts 1995, 223).

Signature marks were made with the tips of the fingers on the top surface of tiles before firing. The marks are believed to have been made by the individual tilemaker, presumably as a way of identifying the work of each tiler and as a check on the number made. The vast majority of signature marks found on the 25 Cannon Street tiles are of semicircular type, with between one and four semicircles. A few tiles do have other types of signature marks, mostly in the form of a one-fingered cross or a two-fingered loop, both of which are known from other London tiles.

Tally marks, added to the tiles during the manufacturing process, were noted on two tegulae. That in [303] (fabric group 2815, type 3006) comprises a single knife-cut in the outer edge of the flange (type ?13). The other is a 'I I' in the same position in a reduced tile of uncertain fabric ([158]).

A number of tiles have other markings in the tile surface added before firing (Fig 50). The most unusual is a tegula <253> (fabric 3016 [926]) which has a number of parallel ridges. This could perhaps be the edge of a curved stamp, or some kind of decoration, although neither have been found on tiles in fabric 3016 previously.

4.5 Period non-ceramic finds summaries

Jackie Keily

Roman

The Roman finds assemblage is quite small, both numerically and in the range of objects recovered, and is too limited to be able to undertake any functional analysis. The most common material type recovered is glass. Fragments of 33 Roman glass vessels were found, quite a small number in terms of urban excavations in London, and all represented by small fragments. A possible glass cullet dump was recovered from a pit to the north-east of the present site in 1954 (GM213) (Shepherd 1986). The present assemblage produced no evidence for glassworking and the glass was found throughout the site, both spatially and stratigraphically. The lack of industrial material, and the relatively high quantity of glass tableware and finer container vessels, would seem to indicate that this was a residential area with a certain degree of wealth rather than industrial.

Only one extremely fragmentary brooch, two hairpins (as well as another shaft fragment) and two glass beads were found <158> <89> (see Fig 16): little that could indicate much about the people who inhabited the buildings on the site. Apart from the glass, there was little evidence for the status of the households or the types of activities undertaken in them: a plain iron handle, a small fragment of a shale bowl, part of a quernstone and a lionhead mount <66> (see Fig 16). The latter have been found decorating burial caskets, but were probably used elsewhere as well.

The most interesting Roman accessioned find is the fragment of stone mould <141> found residually in a Saxo-

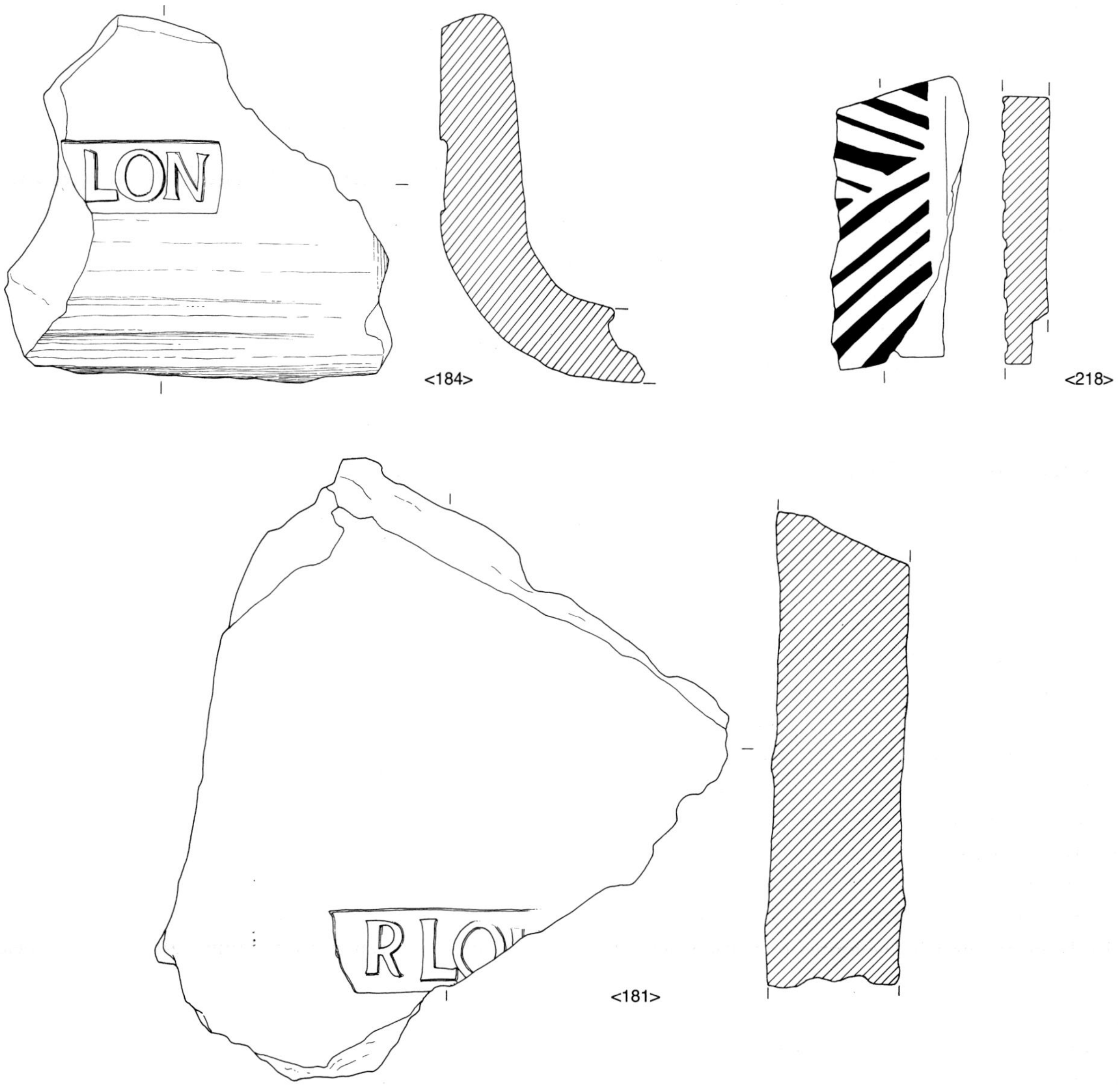

Fig 49 Roman imbrex tile with procuratorial stamp <184>, brick with procuratorial stamp <181> and roller-stamped box-flue tile with possible new die stamp <218> (1:2)

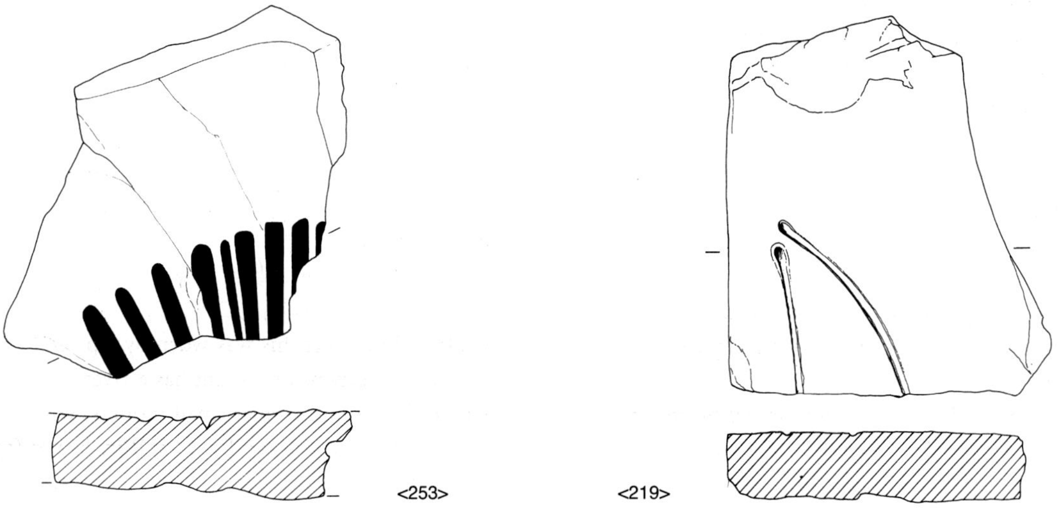

Fig 50 Tegula with unusual surface impression <253> from Building 7, and tegula with graffiti <219> from make-up dumps in Open Area 12 (1:2)

Norman timber-lined cellar (see 2.6 above for discussion and Figs 21–2). No waste pieces, part-made objects or ingots were found associated with it.

Saxon

Little evidence was found for Saxon activity, with the exception of the fragment of Roman brick reused as an ingot mould <215>, found with residual pottery dating to AD 900–1150 (see 2.8 above for discussion and Fig 31). A small fragment of glass is also thought to be Late Saxon in date, probably dating to the 10th–12th centuries (John Shepherd, pers comm).

Medieval and post-medieval

As with the Roman accessioned finds, the metal objects from the medieval period are in a very poor condition. There are, however, some tantalising insights into the wealth of the area in the medieval period (see Fig 37). The corroded small suspension mount with gilded pendant <51> would have been a very fine object worn by a person with some degree of wealth. A small mount with a flower <19> decorating it is similar to other mounts found in London and was probably a more mass-produced object. The small knife handle <5> would also originally have been quite a fine object, although now it is corroded and has been burned.

The most outstanding finds are the glass, including both fine imported drinking vessels and more mundane objects such as bottles, lamps and urinals. The former provides evidence for a household or households of some wealth in the area. One of the most interesting pieces is <138>, a fine, high-quality stemmed drinking glass, possibly imported from Italy (see 2.10 above and Fig 37). Another rare find is a rim fragment from the bowl of a colourless stemmed drinking vessel <134> with trails of thin opaque white glass (see 2.10 above and Fig 37). Part of a colourless *coupelle* with a blue trail was found during recent excavations at Charterhouse (PRR98) (Blackmore in prep).

Other objects associated with households and probably used in the preparation of foodstuffs are the fragments of quern (see 2.9 above) and part of a Purbeck marble mortar. Although more everyday items, they are of interest as they indicate the sorts of objects, even quite everyday ones, which were imported into London. The mortar is part of a trade in stone vessels from Purbeck in Dorset largely during the 13th and 14th centuries. Two hone stones were also found, in a schist-type stone probably imported from northern Europe. The only evidence for industrial activities are the crucible fragments and a single fragment each of copper-alloy waste and iron slag, too little to be able to infer any centre of activity on the site.

The post-medieval period is represented by very few artefacts. A spindlewhorl <43> made of Raeren Stoneware dates to the late 15th or 16th century and was imported from the Rhineland. A plain ivory handle <48> dates to the 18th century and probably comes from a knife. It was found in a brick-lined cesspit with an 18th-century stemmed drinking glass <187> (see 2.12 above and Fig 43).

4.6 Catalogue of the illustrated finds

Jackie Keily

Glass cup: Fig 51
<94> [812] period 5, B20
Translucent dark green; part of a small cup with an out-turned rim with rounded edge; surfaces dull with grinding and polishing marks; a very early and uncommon form; Tiberian/Neronian; *c* AD 20–60.

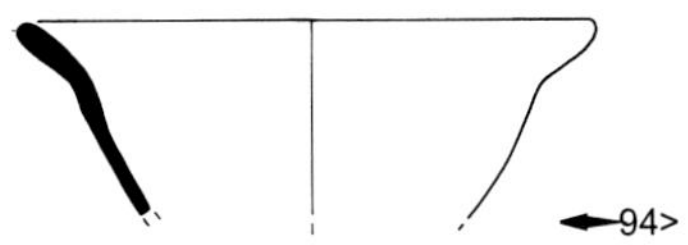

Fig 51 Part of a small cast cup in translucent dark green glass, with an out-turned rim <94>, of Tiberian–Neronian date (c AD 20–60), but recovered from make-up from period 5 (1:2)

Glass bead: Fig 16
<89> [913] period 4, OA13
Complete; L 17mm, Diam 22mm. Dark turquoise melon bead; Roman.

Copper-alloy mount: Fig 16
<66> [775] period 4, OA13
Incomplete; Diam 17.5mm, H 11mm. A lionhead stud with a stylised lion's head in relief; corroded, no trace of the shaft, although there appears to be iron corrosion on the reverse. This type of mount dates to the 1st century AD and is often found associated with the lock plates of burial caskets (Wardle 1993, 96, no. 167).

Copper-alloy mount: Fig 37
<51> [303] period 9, OA27
Incomplete; surviving L 43mm. A small suspension mount with the remains of a fragmentary and very corroded pendant; too little remains of the pendant to be able to identify its form. The front of the pendant appears to be gilded and some decoration is visible but its form is indistinct due to the corrosion. The gilding and decoration, however, would indicate that this was worn by a person of some wealth. The suspension mount has a rivet projecting *c* 7mm behind the mount. Similar small mounts, with and without their pendants, have been found at Winchester (eg Hinton 1990, 1051, fig 336 no. 3916 and 1052, fig 337 no. 3931). The size of the object and its decoration would indicate that it was used for personal ornament; 13th/14th century.

Copper-alloy knife: Fig 37
<5> [182] period 9, S3
Incomplete; surviving L 57mm, maximum W 15mm, Th 4mm. A scale-tang knife handle with wooden scales either side of an iron tang and a copper-alloy end cap. The scales expand slightly towards the end, which is rounded and has four small copper-alloy rivets arranged in a diamond. The wood is very decayed and one area of the middle appears to be burned; the metalwork is very corroded; 15th/16th century.

Stemmed drinking glass: Fig 37
<134> [182] period 9, S3
Two fragments from the bowl of a colourless stemmed drinking glass with a plain rim; the rounded body of the bowl has applied and marvered trails of thin opaque white glass; probably from southern France; 14th/15th century.

Stemmed drinking vessel: Fig 37
<138> [182] period 9, S3
Fragments of a stemmed drinking vessel, giving a complete profile. Greyish-colourless with a hollow, ribbed knop, rounded bowl and tapering hollow base. A very high-quality vessel dating to the late 15th/16th century. This is possibly an imported Italian vessel. The glass itself, however, is not of the finest quality and therefore may be a *façon de Venise* vessel made by Venetian glassworkers in London. The Venetian style of glassmaking was brought to England by a number of Venetian glassworkers who came to London from the late 16th century onward.

Glass lid: Fig 37
<163> [78] period 9, OA28
A mould-blown colourless glass lid with diagonal ribbing; possibly Venetian; 16th/17th century.

Stemmed drinking glass: Fig 43
<187> [57] period 11, B42
Bell bowl, solid inverted baluster stem, base missing; colourless; early 18th century (John Shepherd, pers comm).

Ivory handle: Fig 43
<48> [57] period 11, B42
Incomplete; L 94–97.5mm, W 15–25mm, Th 15–19mm. A plain handle, tapering from an oval, slightly concave, end to a circular section containing the remains of an iron tang. Probably 18th century.

4.7 The animal bones

Alan Pipe

The hand-collected bone fragments were generally in moderate to good surface condition with little difficulty experienced in the identification of species, skeletal element, handedness, modification, ageing evidence or measurement points. Nevertheless, it was found necessary to allocate considerable quantities of bone to the approximate categories 'cattle-sized and sheep-sized' bone and, to lesser degrees, unidentifiable fish, bird and mammal (Table 16; Table 17). The wet-sieved bones were usually in only moderate surface condition with considerable damage noted on the more fragile material, particularly the fish bones. As a result, there was more limited success in identification to species level with this material.

A total of 1690 fragments of animal bone were hand collected from Roman, Late Saxon and early medieval contexts. Table 16 shows the hand-collected species and fragment counts for each period.

A total of 720 fragments of animal bone were recovered from wet-sieved bulk samples from Roman, Late Saxon and early medieval contexts. Table 17 shows the species and fragment counts for each period. The faunal recovery with reference to period and land use has been integrated into the description of the archaeological sequence (Chapter 2).

These fragments derived from a rather narrow range of domestic and wild species which was heavily dominated by ox, with smaller contributions of sheep or goat and pig, with a generally sparse recovery of poultry and very few wild species. The fish derived from true freshwater (roach, cyprinid) and marine (ray, cod, gadid, plaice/flounder, herring, mackerel and gurnard) species with some euryhaline species (smelt, eel and possibly flounder *Platichthys flesus*) tolerant of a range of salinities. The fish were largely represented by small groups of vertebrae, and accurate identification to species level was often impossible as a result. The taxa recovered were elasmobranch (unidentified), ray (probably thornback ray or roker, *Raja clavata*), herring (*Clupea harengus*) and herring family (Clupeidae), smelt (*Osmerus eperlanus*), eel (*Anguilla anguilla*), cod (*Gadus morhua*)

Table 16 Hand-collected animal bone, recovery by period

Species	No. of frags by period						Total
	2	3	4	5	7	8	
cod	0	0	0	0	49	0	**49**
fish, unid	0	0	1	0	0	0	**1**
chicken	2	2	4	13	18	1	**40**
mallard/domestic duck	0	0	0	4	0	0	**4**
goose	0	0	0	0	3	2	**5**
woodcock	0	0	0	0	1	0	**1**
raven	0	0	0	8	0	0	**8**
ox	4	8	28	179	175	49	**443**
'ox-sized'	3	10	23	108	93	14	**251**
sheep/goat	5	1	10	48	72	19	**155**
sheep	2	0	4	7	19	9	**41**
goat	0	0	0	0	1	3	**4**
'sheep-sized'	11	3	28	113	41	5	**201**
pig	7	3	13	202	58	19	**302**
horse	0	0	0	0	28	0	**28**
cat	0	0	0	2	1	0	**3**
dog	0	1	1	136	0	1	**139**
red deer	0	0	0	1	0	0	**1**
roe deer	0	0	0	2	1	0	**3**
mammal, unid	4	0	0	0	7	0	**11**
Total	38	28	112	823	567	122	1690

Table 17 Wet-sieved animal bone, recovery by period

Species	No. of frags by period			Total
	5	**7**	**8**	
elasmobranch	0	1	0	**1**
thornback ray	0	1	0	**1**
Clupeidae	2	0	0	**2**
herring	0	3	0	**3**
smelt	0	5	0	**5**
eel	3	6	0	**9**
Gadidae	31	32	0	**63**
mackerel	0	3	0	**3**
plaice/flounder	17	25	1	**43**
Cyprinidae	0	4	0	**4**
gurnard	0	1	0	**1**
roach	1	0	0	**1**
frog/toad	0	1	0	**1**
chicken	3	2	0	**5**
goose	2	0	0	**2**
woodcock	0	1	0	**1**
bird, passerine	1	1	0	**2**
ox	14	6	0	**20**
'ox-sized'	7	4	0	**11**
sheep/goat	4	130	0	**134**
sheep	1	0	0	**1**
'sheep-sized'	251	39	35	**325**
pig	16	9	1	**26**
roe deer	1	0	0	**1**
dog	49	0	0	**49**
cat	5	0	0	**5**
mammal, unid	1	0	0	**1**
Total	**409**	**274**	**37**	**720**

and cod family (Gadidae), plaice/flounder (Pleuronectidae, probably plaice *Pleuronectes platessa*), roach (*Rutilus rutilus*), carp family (Cyprinidae), mackerel (*Scomber scombrus*) and gurnard (Triglidae).

Amphibians were represented only by a single fragment of frog or toad long bone.

Birds were mainly represented by chicken (*Gallus gallus*) with very much smaller contributions of goose, probably domestic goose (*Anser anser*), and mallard/domestic duck (*Anas platyrhynchos*). The bird fauna also included small unidentified passerines, the carrion and refuse-feeding 'scavenger' species, raven (*Corvus corax*), and the only 'game' bird, woodcock (*Scolopax rusticola*).

Mammals were mainly represented by the major domesticates, particularly ox (*Bos taurus*) with smaller contributions of sheep (*Ovis aries*), goat (*Capra hircus*) and pig (*Sus scrofa*). There was very sparse recovery of wild 'game' mammal species including red deer (*Cervus elaphus*) and roe deer (*Capreolus capreolus*), although it should be stressed that the recovery of antler (red deer and roe deer) and metapodial (roe deer) fragments in the deer remains does not necessarily itself indicate consumption of venison. There was also evidence for disposal of carcasses of working animals with some substantial fragment counts of dog (*Canis familiaris*) and of horse (*Equus caballus*) but only minor recovery of cat (*Felis catus*). There were no small mammals.

FRENCH AND GERMAN SUMMARIES

Résumé

Dans ce rapport, nous présentons les résultats d'une fouille et autres travaux de terrain entrepris au 25 Cannon Street dans la Cité de Londres par le service archéologique du Musée de Londres (Museum of London Archaeological Service, MoLAS) entre 1996 et 1999, code CAO96. Les trouvailles les plus importantes provenant de cette fouille comprennent de la céramique de l'Age de Bronze, des bâtiments de la fin du 1er siècle et quatre bâtiments et leurs sous-sols datant du 11ème siècle. Ce rapport comprend les observations faites par Ivor Noël Hume du Guildhall Museum avant la construction de Gateway House en 1954. Ces observations ont été publiées en 1986 et ont le code GM160. Quelques unes des interprétations faites dans les notes de 1954 sont revues ici à la lumière des nouvelles données. Le centre du site se trouve à la référence nationale TQ 3224 8107.

Les objets les plus anciens trouvés sur ce site sont un ensemble de céramique redéposée (période 1). On a identifié des urnes globulaires et en forme de seau de la tradition Deverel-Rimbury ce qui indique que les environs du site était occupés pendant cette période.

Le site est situé sur les pentes exposées au sud de la colline ouest, l'une des deux sur lesquelles la Cité romaine et les villes suivantes ont été bâties. Pendant les cinq ou dix premières années après la conquête romaine de 43 après J.C., le site se trouvait aux abords peu habités de la nouvelle ville. La phase de construction la plus ancienne sous les romains (période 2) qui n'a peut-être pas pris place avant 60 avant J.C. comprenait aussi des carrières de gravier et d'argile (OA2). L'occupation la plus ancienne est caractérisée par des bâtiments dont les fondations étaient munies de poutres de seuils de portes ou appuis de fenêtres en bois (B1–3), et fut suivie d'une période de développement de plus en plus intense à partir de 70 apr. J.C. marquée par l'introduction de bâtiments en maçonnerie ainsi que de nouvelles structures en bois.

Aux environs de 100 apr. J.C., le premier bâtiment muni de murs en maçonnerie (B100) fut détruit pour être remplacé par une structure plus grande (B10) dont l'orientation était différente de celle des précédentes mais semblable à celle de bâtiments situés 100m plus à l'est. Aux environs de *c.* 140–250 apr. J.C., les constructions dans ce secteur étaient devenues très denses (période 4); certains bâtiments situés du côté est du site possédaient des sols en mosaïque executée assez maladroitement (B14–15). L'orientation continuelle des bâtiments du côté nord du site et à Watling House à l'ouest a servi d'argument pour émettre l'hypothèse qu'il y avait une route romaine au nord, sous Watling Street, un peu plus au nord de ce qui avait été suggéré auparavant.

Un bâtiment du 2ème siècle au moins fut démoli au 3ème siècle pour être remplacé par un bâtiment aux mosaïques très étendues (B21) qui a continué à être utilisé jusqu'à la fin de l'occupation romaine bien qu'avec des réparations de moins en moins bien faites (période 5). Au nord du site, un bâtiment fut construit au 3ème ou 4ème siècle (B20) avec une orientation différente de celle des autres bâtiments ce qui peut indiquer un changement d'orientation de la route si elle existait. Un des objets les plus importants de l'époque romaine est le fragment d'un moule en pierre du 3ème ou 4ème siècle qui, l'on pense, a pu servir à la fabrication d'assiettes décorées en étain. L'abandonnement du site à la fin de l'occupation romaine ne peut être daté d'une façon satisfaisante, mais il est marqué par l'accumulation de terre (dark earth) sur les sols (période 6).

Le site fut réoccupé au 10ème ou au 11ème siècle, et vers le milieu du 11ème siècle quatre bâtiments aux sous-sols revêtus de bois avaient été construits (période 7). Leur construction semble prédater celle de Friday Street et de l'église de St Werburga, plus tard nommée St Jean l'Evangéliste. On a retrouvé dans un des bâtiments deux pots enterrés sous le sol, il s'agit soit d'une offrande soit peut-être d'un objet à but industriel. Deux creusets et une tuile romaine retravaillée en moule pour les lingots de cuivre indiquent une certaine activité d'ordre industriel dans les environs à cette époque.

La datation de Friday Street est douteuse: la surface la plus ancienne de la route que l'on ait pu observer a peut-être été construite à la fin du 11ème siècle, mais elle peut aussi dater d'après 1180 (période 8). Des couches plus anciennes ont sans dout été préservées en-dessous. L'église de St Werburga fut construite entre 1098 et 1108 et reconstruite avec un choeur plus large au 13ème ou au 14ème siècle (B103).

Les bâtiments du Moyen-Age et les constructions plus récentes ont été fortement tronqués par des sous-sols modernes mais l'on a pu malgré tout suggérer que les constructions du Moyen-Age étaient toutes situées en retrait â environ 12,5m le long des deux côtés de Friday Street tout comme les autres bâtiments médiévaux des environs (périodes 8–9). En général, les restes de l'époque médiévale étaient constitués soit d'ordures soit de restes de fosses d'aisance. Certaines de ces dernières furent construites avec des murs en maçonnerie à partir du 13ème siècle.

Les sous-sols et fosses d'aisance indiquent l'existence d'une occupation jusqu'au Grand Feu de 1666 (période 10) qui détruisit la totalité du site. L'église de St Jean l'Evangéliste ne fut pas reconstruite mais le cimetière a continué à être utilisé jusqu'au 19ème siècle (période 11).

Zusammenfassung

Dieser Bericht präsentiert die Ergebnisse der Ausgrabung und vorbereitenden Arbeiten in 25 Cannon Street, City of London, die dort vom Museum of London Archaeology Service zwischen 1996 und 1999 unter dem Ausgrabungscode CAO96 durchgeführt wurden. Als Hauptfunde dieser Ausgrabung kamen Mittlere Bronzezeit Töpferware, Gebäude aus dem späten 1. Jahrhundert und vier weitere unterkellerte aus dem 11. Jahrhundert zutage. Der Bericht enthält auch die Anmerkungen Ivor Noël Humes vom Guildhall Museum, die dieser 1954 vor Beginn der Bauarbeiten am Gateway House machte. Sie wurden schon 1986 von John Shepherd unter dem Ausgrabungscode GM160 veröffentlicht. Einige dieser Interpretationen wurden im Lichte der neuen Befunde revidiert. Das Zentrum der Ausgrabung liegt im nationalen Vermessungsnetz bei TQ 3224 8107.

Der früheste archäologische Fund bestand aus einer Gruppe redeponierter Töpferware aus der Mittleren Bronzezeit (Periode 1). Identifizierung eines Kübels und einer kugelförmigen Urne im Deverel-Rimbury-Stil weisen auf Besiedlung der Gegend während dieser Zeit hin.

Die Ausgrabungsstätte liegt auf dem Südhang des westlichen zweier Hügel, auf denen die römische und die spätere Stadt gebaut wurde. Während der ersten fünf bis zehn Jahre nach der Eroberung durch die Römer in 43 n. Chr. lag sie am damals noch nicht voll genutzten Rande der neuen Stadt. Während der frühesten Phase römischer Bautätigkeit (Periode 2), die nicht vor 60 n. Chr. begonnen haben mag, wurden dort Kies und Ton gewonnen (OA2). Für die frühe Siedlungstätigkeit waren Gebäude mit hölzernen Fundamentbalken typisch (B1–3). Ihr folgte von *c* 70 n. Chr. an zunehmend dichtere Besiedlung (Periode 3), als neben neuen Holzkonstruktionen auch Steinbauten entstanden.

Um 100 n. Chr. wurde das erste Steingebäude (B100) abgerissen, um einem größeren Gebäude (B10) Platz zu machen, dessen Ausrichtung nicht mit dem früheren, wohl aber mit den Gebäuden etwa 100m östlich übereinstimmte. In der Zeit von 140–250 war die Gegend schon dicht bebaut (Periode 4), wobei einige der Bauten auf der Ostseite, wenn auch relativ primitive so doch Mosaikfußböden enthielten (B14, B15). Die einheitliche Ausrichtung der Gebäude auf der Nordseite und bei Watling House im Osten hat zu der Hypothese geführt, daß unmittelbar nördlich unterhalb Watling Street aber ein wenig nördlicher als früher angenommen, eine römische Straße vorbeiführte.

Wenigstens eines der Gebäude aus dem 2. Jahrhundert wurde im 3. Jahrhundert abgerissen, um einem Gebäude mit ausgedehnten Mosaikfußböden Platz zu machen (B21). Dieses Gebäude stand bis zum Ende der römischen Besetzung (Periode 5), wenn auch die Qualität der Reparaturarbeiten nachließ. Auf der Nordseite der Ausgrabung wurde im 3. oder 4. Jahrhundert ein Gebäude errichtet (B20), dessen Ausrichtung sich von anderen Bauten unterschied. Der Grund hierfür mag eine Verlegung der hypothetischen Straße gewesen sein. Unter den römischen Funden war eine aus dem 3. oder 4. Jahrhundert stammende steinerne Gußform bemerkenswert, die der Herstellung verzierter Zinnteller gedient haben mag. Die Aufgabe der Siedlung am Ende der römischen Besetzung kann nicht zureichend datiert werden, ist aber durch 'Dark Earth' gekennzeichnet (Periode 6), die sich auf den Böden ansammelte.

Die Wiederbesiedlung begann im 10. oder 11. Jahrhundert und um die Mitte des 11. Jahrhunderts standen dort vier Gebäude mit holzverschalten Kellern (Periode 7). Ihre Errichtung fand offensichtlich früher statt als die Bebauung von Friday Street und als der Bau der St Werburga-, der späteren Johanneskirche. Unter dem Fußboden eines der Gebäude lagen zwei heile Töpfe begraben, die entweder für ein Opfer oder für industrielle Zwecke benutzt worden waren. Zwei Tiegel und ein als Gußform für das Gießen von Barren aus Kupferlegierung umgearbeiteter römischer Ziegel bezeugen den Grad der industriellen Aktivität in der Nachbarschaft während dieser Zeit.

Die Datierung der Friday Street ist ungewiß: Der früheste Straßenbelag mag im späten 11. Jahrhundert aufgebracht worden sein, aber er mag auch nach 1180 (Periode 8) datieren. Frühere Lagen darunter mögen *in situ* erhalten sein. Die St Werburga-Kirche wurde zwischen 1098 und 1108 errichtet und dann im 13. oder 14. Jahrhundert mit einem breiteren Altarraum umgebaut (B103).

Die Überreste mittelalterlicher und späterer Gebäude wurden von modernen Fundamenten stark beschädigt, lassen aber erkennen, daß die frühmittelalterlichen Gebäude beiderseits der Friday Street, ähnlich denen anderer mittelalterlicher Gebäude in der Nachbarschaft, eine Tiefe von etwa 12.5m von der Straße entfernt erreichten (Periode 8–9). Die Mehrheit der mittelalterlichen Funde bestanden aus Abfall und Klärgruben. Einige der letzteren wurden vom 13. Jahrhundert an mit Steinmauern eingefaßt.

Keller und weitere Klärgruben bezeugen Besiedlung bis zum großen Feuer 1666 (Periode 10), das die ganze Anlage zerstörte. Die Johanneskirche wurde nicht wieder aufgebaut, aber der Friedhof wurde als Begräbnisstätte bis zum 19. Jahrhundert benutzt (Periode 11).

BIBLIOGRAPHY

Place of publication given for books published outside the United Kingdom.

Arnold, H R, 1994 *Atlas of mammals in Britain*, Institute of Terrestrial Ecology Res Pub 6

Atkinson, D R, and Oswald, A, 1969 London clay tobacco pipes, *J Brit Archaeol Ass* 32

Barrett, J C, 1973 Four Bronze Age cremation cemeteries from Middlesex, *Trans London Middlesex Archaeol Soc* 24, 111–34

Beagrie, N, 1989 The Romano-British pewter industry, *Britannia* 20, 169–91

Beer, E de (ed), 1955 *The diary of John Evelyn: Vol 3, 1650–72*

Betts, I M, 1994 Medieval floor tiles in London churches, in Saxon and medieval parish churches in the City of London: a review (ed J Schofield), *Trans London Middlesex Archaeol Soc* 45, 133–40

Betts, I M, 1995 Procuratorial tile stamps from London, *Britannia* 26, 207–29

Betts, I M, in prep *Medieval 'Westminster' floor tiles*, MoLAS Monogr Ser

Blackmore, L, 1994 Pottery, the port and the populace: the imported pottery of London 1300–1600 (Part 1), *Medieval Ceram* 18, 29–44

Blackmore, L, 1999a Aspects of trade and exchange evidenced by recent work on Saxon and medieval pottery from London, in Medieval London: recent archaeological work and research, *Trans London Middlesex Archaeol Soc* 50, 38–54

Blackmore, L, 1999b Commerce and the capital: archaeological aspects of London's trade 1100–1700, in *Lübecker Kolloquium zur Stadtarchäologie im Hanseraum II: der Handel* (ed M Gläser), Lübeck, 37–58

Blackmore, L, in prep Shelly Sandy ware, in *Medieval coarsewares of the London area: a dated type-series of London medieval pottery: Part 5, Shelly Sandy ware and the Greyware industries* (L Blackmore and J Pearce)

Blake, H, 1999 'De nomine Jhesu': an Italian export ware and the origin of Renaissance maiolica pottery making in the Netherlands, in Gaimster 1999, 23–56

Boon, G C, 1974 *Silchester: the Roman town of Calleva*

Bowsher, D, 1999, 40–43 Bow Lane and 70–71 Watling Street, an archaeological evaluation, unpub MoLAS rep

Britton, F, 1987 *London delftware*

Cotton, J, 1981 Bronze Age pottery from Wood Lane, Osterley, *Trans London Middlesex Archaeol Soc* 32, 18–23

Cotton, J, 1993 Excavations and observations of a Bronze Age cemetery and Roman site in Avenue Gardens, Acton, Middlesex, 1882 and 1981–5, *Trans London Middlesex Archaeol Soc* 44, 1–22

Culpeper, N, 1653 *The complete herbal*

Davis, A, in prep a The plant remains, in *Excavations at Regis House, 1994–96* (eds T Brigham and B Watson), MoLAS Monogr Ser

Davis, A, in prep b The plant remains, in *Excavations at 1 Poultry: Vol 1, The Roman sequence* (eds J Hill and P Rowsome), MoLAS Monogr Ser

Eames, E S, 1980 *Catalogue of medieval lead-glazed earthenware tiles in the Department of Medieval and Later Antiquities British Museum*

English Heritage, 1991 *Management of archaeological projects*

Flower, B, and Rosenbaum, E (trans), 1958 *The Roman cookery book: a critical translation of The Art of Cooking by Apicius*
Gaimster, D (ed), 1999 *Maiolica in the North: the archaeology of tin-glazed earthenware in north-west Europe c 1500–1600*, British Museum Occ Pap 122
Gentleman's Magazine, 1833 Reviews, *The Gentleman's Magazine, and Historical Chronicle* 103, Part 2
Grieve, M, 1994 (1931) *A modern herbal*
Harben, H, 1918 *A dictionary of the City of London*
Hill, J, and Woodger, A, 1999 *Excavations at 72–75 Cheapside/83–93 Queen Street, City of London*, MoLAS Archaeol Stud Ser 2
Hohler, C, 1942 Medieval paving tiles from Buckinghamshire, *Rec Buckinghamshire* 14, 1–49, 99–132
Horsman, V, Milne, C, and Milne, G, 1988 *Aspects of Saxo-Norman London: 1, Building and street development near Billingsgate and Cheapside*, London Middlesex Archaeol Soc Spec Pap 11
Huelin, G, 1996 *Vanished churches of the City of London*
Hughes, M, and Gaimster, D, 1999 Neutron activation analysis of maiolica from London, Norwich, the Low Countries and Italy, in Gaimster 1999, 57–91
Hurst, J G, 1977 Spanish pottery imported into medieval Britain, *Medieval Archaeol* 21, 68–105
Hurst, J G, Neal, D S, and van Beuningen, H J E, 1986 *Pottery produced and traded in north-west Europe 1350–1650*, Rotterdam Pap 6
Keily, J, 1997 Assessment of the post-Roman accessioned finds from the Guildhall excavations: GDH85, GAG87 and GYE92, unpub MoLAS rep
Keys, L, 1998 Glass urinals, in *The medieval household, daily living c 1150–c 1450*, Medieval finds from excavations in London 6 (ed G Egan)
Lack, P, 1993 *The atlas of wintering birds in Britain and Ireland*
Lakin, D, 1997 Junction of Cannon Street and Bread Street, EC4, City of London, an archaeological watching brief, unpub MoLAS rep
Lobel, M D, 1989 *The British atlas of historic towns: 3, The City of London from prehistoric times to c 1520*
Mabey, R, 1977 *Plants with a purpose: a guide to the everyday uses of wild plants*
Maloney, C, 1980 A witch bottle from Duke's Place, Aldgate, *Trans London Middlesex Archaeol Soc* 31, 157–8
Marsden, P, 1968 Archaeological finds in the City of London, 1965–6, *Trans London Middlesex Archaeol Soc* 22, Part 1, 1–17
Marsden, P, and West, B, 1992 Population change in Roman London, *Britannia* 23, 133–40
Marsden, P, Dyson, T, and Rhodes, M, 1975 Excavations on the site of St Mildred's Church, Bread Street, London, 1973–1974, *Trans London Middlesex Archaeol Soc* 26, 171–208
Marsh, G, and Tyers, P A, 1978 The Roman pottery from Southwark, in *Southwark excavations 1972–74* (eds J Bird, A H Graham, H Sheldon and P Townend), London Middlesex Archaeol Soc/Surrey Archaeol Soc, joint pub 1
Merrifield, R, 1965 *The Roman city of London*
Merrifield, R, 1969 Folklore in London archaeology: Part 2, Post-Roman period, *London Archaeol* 1(5), 99–104
Merriman, N, 1987 A prehistory for central London?, *London Archaeol* 5(12), 318–26
MoLAS, 1997 West London landscape project: assessment and updated project design, unpub MoLAS rep
Moorhouse, S, 1972 Medieval distilling-apparatus of glass and pottery, *Medieval Archaeol* 16, 79–121
Moorhouse, S, 1981 The medieval pottery industry and its markets, in *Medieval industry* (ed D W Crossley), CBA Res Rep 40, 96–125
Noël Hume, I, 1977 *Early English delftware from London and Virginia*, Colonial Williamsburg Occ Pap in Archaeol 3
Peacock, D P S, and Williams, D F, 1986 *Amphorae and the Roman economy: an introductory guide*
Pearce, J, 1992 *Post-medieval pottery in London 1500–1700: Vol 1, Border wares*
Pearce, J, and Vince, A, 1988 *A dated type-series of London medieval pottery: Part 4, Surrey Whitewares*, London Middlesex Archaeol Soc Spec Pap 10
Pearce, J E, Vince, A G, and Jenner, M A, 1985 *A dated type-series of London medieval pottery: Part 2, London-type ware*, London Middlesex Archaeol Soc Spec Pap 6
Perring, D, 1991 *Roman London*
Perring, D, and Roskams, S, with Allen, P, 1991 *The archaeology of Roman London: Vol 2, The early development of Roman London west of the Walbrook*, CBA Res Rep 70
Pipe, A, in prep Animal bone, in *Industry in north-west Roman Southwark: excavations at Courage's Brewery, 1984–8* (ed F Hammer), MoLAS Monogr Ser
Price, J, and Cottam, S, 1998 *Romano-British glass vessels: a handbook*, CBA Practical Handbook in Archaeology 14
Pritchard, F, 1991 Small finds, in *Aspects of Saxo-Norman London: 2, Finds and environmental evidence* (ed A Vince), London Middlesex Archaeol Soc Spec Pap 12
Rayner, L, in prep The prehistoric pottery, in *Roman and medieval Cripplegate: recent excavations* (eds E Howe and D Lakin), MoLAS Monogr Ser
RCHME, 1928 Roy Comm Hist Monuments Engl, *An inventory of the historical monuments in London: Vol 3, Roman London*
Sabben, C van, and Hollem, J, 1987 *Antieke tegels*, Haarlem
Schofield, J, 1994 Saxon and medieval parish churches in the City of London: a review, *Trans London Middlesex Archaeol Soc* 45, 23–146
Schofield, J, Allen, P, and Taylor, C, 1990 Medieval buildings and property development in the area of Cheapside, *Trans London Middlesex Archaeol Soc* 41, 39–237
Sharrock, J T R, 1987 *The atlas of breeding birds in Britain and Ireland*
Shepherd, J D, 1986 The Roman features at Gateway House and Watling House, Watling Street, City of London (1954), *Trans London Middlesex Archaeol Soc* 37, 125–44
Sidell, J, Cotton, J, Rayner, L, and Wheeler, L, in prep *The topography and prehistory of Southwark and Lambeth*, MoLAS Monogr Ser
Thomas, C, Cowie, R, and Sidell, J, in prep *Excavations at Thorney Island, Westminster: archaeological excavations (1991–8) for the London Underground Limited Jubilee Line Extension Project*, MoLAS Monogr Ser
Vince, A G, 1985 Saxon and medieval pottery in London: a review, *Medieval Archaeol* 29, 25–93
Vince, A, and Jenner, A, 1991 The Saxon and early medieval

pottery of London, in *Aspects of Saxo-Norman London: 2, Finds and environmental evidence* (ed A Vince), London Middlesex Archaeol Soc Spec Pap 12

Wardle, A, with Pritchard, F, 1993 Accessioned finds, in Early Roman development at Leadenhall Court (eds G Milne and A Wardle), *Trans London Middlesex Archaeol Soc* 44, 23–169

Watson, B, 1998, 'Dark earth' and urban decline in late Roman London, in *Roman London: recent archaeological work* (ed B Watson), *J Roman Archaeol* supp ser 24

Willcox, G H, 1977 Exotic plants from Roman waterlogged sites in London, *J Archaeol Sci* 4, 269–82

Yalden, D, 1999 *The history of British mammals*

INDEX

Compiled by Susanne Atkin

Page numbers in **bold** refer to illustrations